Growing With My Garden

GROWING WITH MY GARDEN

THOUGHTS ON TENDING THE SOIL AND THE SOUL

ROLLAND HEIN

WIPF & STOCK · Eugene, Oregon

Wipf and Stock Publishers
199 W 8th Ave, Suite 3
Eugene, OR 97401

Growing With My Garden
Thoughts on Tending the Soil and Soul
By Hein, Rolland
Copyright©2004 by Hein, Rolland
ISBN 13: 978-1-62564-383-4
Publication date 1/7/2014
Previously published by Cornerstone Press, 2004

To Dorothy

My wife and gardening companion

. . . and what's the earth
With all its art, verse, music, worth—
Compared with love, found, gained, and kept?

— Robert Browning

Other books by Rolland Hein:

Life Essential: The Hope of the Gospel, ed.

Creation in Christ: The Unspoken Sermons of George MacDonald, ed.

George MacDonald's World: An Anthology from the Novels, ed.

The Miracles of Our Lord, ed.

The Harmony Within: The Spiritual Vision of George MacDonald

George MacDonald: Victorian Mythmaker

The Heart of George MacDonald, ed.

Christian Mythmakers: C.S. Lewis, Madeleine L'Engle, J.R.R. Tolkien, George MacDonald, G. K. Chesterton & others, 2nd Edition.

LISTING OF CHAPTERS

Introduction 1

Chapters

1	Let's Make It New	7
2	Planning the Work; Working the Plan	13
3	Problems with Paths	19
4	Let It Be	27
5	What about Tilth?	31
6	Seeds Grow, but Who Knows How?	37
7	Give Up and Give Over	43
8	Nature Is Never Spent	49
9	Why Not Simply Pull It Out?	55
10	A Smile on All Creation	61
11	Those Terrible Choices	67
12	Therefore I Have Hope	73
13	Showers of Blessing	77
14	Reality	81
15	The Moments Satan Cannot Find	87
16	Waiting for the Harvest	91
17	Out of Evil, Good	99
18	What I Do Is Me	105
19	Winter Doldrums	111
20	Putting on the Beauty	119
21	The Unimaginable Zero Summer	125

> *. . . the first thing the casual critic will say is "What nonsense all this is; do you mean that a poet cannot be thankful for grass and wild flowers without connecting it with theology; let alone your theology?"*
>
> *To which I answer, "Yes; I mean he cannot do it without connecting it with theology, unless he can do it without connecting it with thought."*
>
> —G. K. Chesterton

> *The plant does not have any control or choice in the matter of its own growth. As for us, we are like plants that have the one choice of being in or out of the light.*
>
> —Simone Weil

INTRODUCTION

In the middle of a bed of magenta geraniums and golden coreopsis a wrought-iron plaque offers the verse:

> *The kiss of the sun for pardon*
> *The song of the birds for mirth;*
> *One is nearer God's heart in the garden*
> *Than anywhere on earth.*

Doggerel, yes, but it's true: in my garden, more than any other place, I feel something of the presence of God. To say so is not to reduce Him to the life of trees and plants. He is not an amorphous deity but the living God, the Ultimate Person, the ineffable One who inhabits eternity, whose name is Holy. He is the Great Creator: He called into being all things, and in Him everything finds its purpose and reason for being. There is no place where He is not, but there are some places where He can be more quickly felt, a garden preeminent among them.

The Bible suggests as much. When God first made man and woman, He put them in a garden, telling them to tend it, and in the cool of the evening He looked for them there. John tells us Christ was accustomed to meeting His disciples in a garden. In His darkest hour before the cross He went to a garden to pray, His body was laid in a garden tomb, and it was in that garden on the first Easter morning that the astounding truth of the Resurrection began to dawn upon the disciples. Mary mistook the Risen Christ to be a gardener. When the Hebrew prophets express their vision of a fully redeemed and restored society—that future state in which redeemed people will be fully "at home" and content—they picture it like a "well-watered garden."

"I come to the garden alone, while the dew is still on the roses," a familiar hymn relates, "and He walks with me, and He talks with me, and He tells me I am His own." Romantic sentiment to many, perhaps, but happy is the person who finds such an experience to be a precious part of life. The beauty in nature has been placed there by God as a means of calling our attention to Himself. Simone Weil observes that since a genuine love of our fellow beings and of religious practices is almost entirely absent from people today, "the beauty of the world is almost the only way by which we can allow God to penetrate us." Speaking of beauty in its totality, she continues:

> The beauty of the world is the co-operation of divine wisdom in creation. "Zeus made all things," says an Orphic line, "and Bacchus perfected them." This perfecting is the creation of beauty; God created the universe, and his Son, our first-born brother, created the beauty of it for us. The beauty of the world is Christ's tender smile for us coming through matter. He is really present in the universal

INTRODUCTION

beauty. The love of this beauty proceeds from God dwelling in our souls and goes out to God present in the universe. It also is like a sacrament. (*Waiting for God*, 102-4)

As we meet God's Spirit in nature He nurtures and enhances the joys of life, He strengthens our spirit and we find wisdom to face our difficulties.

Whether I'm planting bulbs, pulling weeds, or picking berries, my mind seldom dwells long upon the repetitious movements I'm making. Rather, it is preoccupied with the affairs of my life. I may be wrestling with a particular problem or planning some activity or considering the implications of some idea. Anything can and should be shared with the Spirit of God, and I can do it there. Solutions and inspirations come in an atmosphere of peace and an aura of joy.

If this line of thought seems curiously out of harmony with the ideals promoted by our materialistic age of fast-paced busyness, artificial intelligence, and genetic engineering, perhaps we need to rethink what it means to be truly human. Because God created nature as the best context for man, it would seem wise to consider our humanity in terms of it. The breathtaking intricacies and unfathomable mysteries of earthly life all have their source in His divine ingenuity, and their wonders increase our awe of Him. The natural world is ideally suited for our true needs. Great wisdom lies in being rightly related to it.

The Bible states that "by faith we understand that the world was created by the word of God, so that what is seen was made out of things which do not appear" (Heb. 11:3, *Revised Standard Version*). Things unseen are ever trying to come to us through things seen; their readiest vehicles are found in the garden—its flowers, its fruits, its forms. The person without faith sees only the things that do appear; the person of faith sees nature informed and shaped by things that do not appear, the spiritual realities that have a direct relationship with one's inner being. "A fool sees not the same tree that a wise man sees," William Blake wisely observed. (*The Complete Poetry and Prose of William Blake*, 35)

One way the unseen world communicates to us is by offering a myriad of metaphors for living. For instance, a dahlia as a young plant has within it the promise of a glorious bloom, the final expression of its unique nature; but that promise will be realized only as I give it the nurture and care that will take it successfully through its various phases of growth and development until at last it buds and flowers. Removing redundant buds and lateral branches must surely be distressing if not painful to the plant, while watering and fertilizing encourage it to do its best. The plant must know both joy and apparent hurt, all necessary for it to produce its best bloom. Is this not the way with every human being? William Blake wrote:

Joy and woe are woven fine,
A clothing for the soul divine
Under every grief and pine
Runs a joy with silken twine
It is right it should be so
Man was made for joy and woe
And when this we rightly know
Through the world we safely go.
(Ibid., 494-95)

Any goals a person pursues require discipline and invariably involve self-denial. No life is without pain. God as the Great Gardener of our souls prunes our natures and sends us circumstances designed to bring out our best. This is a book about the truths my garden has shown me of God, of life, and of myself and how I have grown with my garden.

CHAPTER ONE
LET'S MAKE IT NEW

As I sit at my study window, I look southward some sixty feet past a Norway maple and down a gentle slope of lawn to Knoll Creek that serpentines its way from west to east the length of our property. Our ranch house sits parallel to the creek and not quite at the top of the knoll, which means several of our flower beds are on an incline. The beds are recent.

We've lived here only a few years, since I retired from full-time teaching. The previous owners were not gardeners; while they kept the lawn nicely trimmed, they also allowed an odd assortment of brush and trees, mainly wild cherry, mulberry, and willow, to grow at random and flourish, especially along the creek. Some areas were so choked with undergrowth that walking through them in the height of summer was simply unthinkable.

The challenge was exciting. I have been fanatical about gardening all my life, and here was an opportunity to begin afresh during my retirement years and build one final garden, turning a relatively neglected tract into a satisfying landscape by indulging more fully my love for plants and shrubs. Formerly, time for gardening had been limited by the demands of my work. It was an avocation. Now I had liberty to do as much as my body would still allow.

Tree removal came first. The smallest ones and the brush I tackled myself, with axe and adz, felling trunks and removing roots. A tree service handled the larger ones, giving us fireplace wood for years to come.

Next came the sod. A person has two options. The one is to spray on a vegetation killer, wait two weeks until all the vegetation is dead, and then proceed with spading and tilling. The other is to remove the sod live, either with a mechanized sod roller, available at any rental store, or with a hand tool designed especially for that purpose. I tried both and came to prefer the latter method. With spraying I discovered that even though one gets a good "kill," some grass roots may remain to grow among the flowers the following year, much to one's annoyance. Grass is difficult to eradicate by weeding. The dead turf is also very difficult to till under without first spading the bed, one of the more backbreaking tasks of gardening.

Rototilling followed. After I added soil conditioners, the tiller tines sank nicely into the loamy virgin soil, pulverizing it to a fine consistency. I was well on my way to making our landscape new.

Making things new is really what Christianity is all about. As St. John nears the conclusion to his great apocalyptic vision, he hears God say "Behold, I make all things new" (Rev. 21:5). The astonishing statement stands as a great concluding pronouncement that identifies God's overarching intention; how He is accomplishing His task may be said to be the primary theme of the entire Bible.

His first concern is to introduce the reality of eternal life—life clean and pure and filled with hope—into each individual's consciousness. "If any one is in Christ, he is a new creation; the old has passed away, behold, the new has come" (2 Cor. 5:17). William Law puts it well:

> This is the sole end of Christianity: to lead us from all thoughts of rest and repose here, to separate us from worldly tempers, to deliver us from the folly of

> our passions, and to unite us to God, the true fountain of all good. The mighty change which Christianity aims at, then, is to put us into a new state, reform our whole natures, purify our souls and make them the inhabitants of heavenly and immortal bodies.
> (A *Practical Treatise on Christian Perfection*, 23)

The inner life of the individual who has not truly met God in Christ may well be like the unkept lot with its rank undergrowth that cries out to be cleared away and its random junk trees that serve no pleasing or constructive purpose. Saying yes to God is like engaging an expert landscape artist who will, if given a free hand, work to transform one's life into a thing of beauty in his sight.

The old, natural life with its base desires is not easily dealt with, certainly, and negative thoughts still pass through the mind; but the former inner life is in the process of dying and the new is overcoming it. One recognizes temptations for what they are but, no longer comfortable with contemptible thoughts, gives attention to what is good and true and positive. The certain evidence that the Spirit of God is working within to effect renewal is the discomfort one feels in the presence of what formerly was enjoyable and the urge to have no more to do with it.

God's intention to make all things new includes His breathtaking promise to create new heavens and earth. Like undeveloped landscapes that cry out to be beautified, this fallen world, with all its problems and trials and heartaches, cries out to be remade. God has placed us here to learn to work together with Him by learning to love as He loves. The world itself is the most appropriate school. "Earth's the right place for love: / I don't know where it's likely to grow better" (Frost, *Complete Poems, Prose, & Plays*, 118). To respond is to make a difference both in the world around one's self and in the world within. Strength and wisdom to meet the experiences of each day are promised to those who commit themselves to these high goals.

God will, in His own time and manner, complete the work of recreating heaven and earth for redeemed humanity. "According to his promise we wait for new heavens and a new earth in which righteousness dwells" (2 Peter 3:13). What will it be like? I cannot but think the natural world will not be that different from that which we now know but with all disease and deformities removed. "I consider that the sufferings of this present time are not worth comparing with the glory that is to be revealed to us. For the creation waits with eager longing for the revealing of the sons of God . . . . because the creation itself will be set free from its bondage to decay and obtain the glorious liberty of the children of God." (Rom. 8:18, 19, 21). The prospect is glorious. The prospect is glorious. A fine old hymn speaks of the effect of such hope upon one's spirit:

> *My life flows on in endless song*
> *above earth's lamentation.*
> *I hear the real though distant song*
> *that hails a new creation.*
> *Through all the tumult and the strife*
> *I hear the music ringing.*
> *It sounds an echo in my soul,*
> *how can I keep from singing?*

In some mysterious way, making a new garden, spurred on by the hopes and dreams of approximating a corner of Eden, can be a humble type of what God is in the process of making happen in individual lives and in the entire universe.

CHAPTER TWO
PLANNING THE WORK; WORKING THE PLAN

I began landscaping our new place by trying to imagine what I wanted the entire site to look like when finished. Then I took a sketch pad and measuring tape—at first I hesitated to spend the money for that hundred-foot roll, then splurged, and have been glad ever since that I did—and measured and roughly sketched the targeted areas. Someone told me to note the amount of sunlight or degree of shade each section receives, remembering that these patterns are different under a January sun than under a June one.

Excellent advice. Perhaps nothing is as important in the planning and planting stages as siting plants correctly, and the amount of sunshine a spot receives is the most crucial factor. Often moving a plant just a few feet will help it perform quite differently. Morning sunshine is preferable to afternoon; a site that has full morning sun and partial shade in the afternoon is ideal for most sun-loving plants. But if your site is in full shade, do not despair; you can still have a flower garden that is the marvel of the neighborhood. Simply plan to use plants that need shade, such as impatiens, coleus, hostas, and caladiums. Your garden center will have many suggestions for you.

The first step is to be realistic in deciding where the garden will be and how much room will be given to it. Bigger is not necessarily better; a smaller plot that is well-planned and cared for will be much more satisfying in July than one too large to be well-kept. Sitting in a warm house on a January day, a person can easily be more ambitious than time or abilities warrant.

Retreating to the warmth of my home, I carefully drew the plot to scale on a large piece of drafting paper and, with those colorful gardening catalogs by my side, proceeded to choose and place plants. Plants must be correctly spaced for happy effects. Recommendations can be found in a good gardening catalog or gardening encyclopedia; I like *Rodale's Encyclopedia of Organic Gardening*. I tried to exercise a prudent eye for plant heights as well as color combinations, remembering from what vantage point the plot would most often be viewed.

Too many colors in one bed are less pleasing than, say, three harmonious ones, but glaring mistakes in color combinations are seldom made. Nature has an uncanny way of blending colors. If a person finds it difficult to visualize different color combinations, a handy trick is to clip pictures of proposed plants from a nursery catalog—one that features colorful pictures of various plants, such as *Wayside Gardens'*—and place them on the garden diagram. It is fun to do, and it also reminds one of the different textures of foliage, together with size and shape of blooms.

One should plan to situate plants in groups of three or five, repeating such clumps at somewhat regular intervals (avoid repetitions that seem too rigid and precise) throughout a given area. A pleasing sense of rhythm is critical in achieving coherence and symmetry. The importance of patient and thorough planning in these matters cannot be overemphasized.

If satisfying gardening requires careful and elaborate planning followed by patient and consistent effort, how much more does a satisfying life. Just as no completed garden looks entirely like the gardener's early plans and imaginings, so the life lived may vary widely from the life intended. Realizing that God, not myself, is the landscape architect of my life is the first step in reducing my dismay when personal plans go awry. He waits to be asked; if I am trusting Him to give me a happy life beyond the grave, I must trust Him to direct my life now. The asking must be sincere and earnest, the trust complete. George MacDonald wrote:

> Everyone must walk by the light given him. By the rules which others have laid down he may learn to walk; but once his heart is awake to truth, and his ear to measure, melody and harmony, he must walk by the light, and the music God gives him. (*The Elect Lady*, 12)

In his poem "Death and Birth" one finds the poignant lines:

> *Find the secret—follow and find!*
> *All forget that lies behind;*
> *Me, the schools, yourselves, forsake;*
> *In your souls a silence make;*
> *Hearken till a whisper come,*
> *Listen, follow, and be dumb.*
> (Poetical Works of George MacDonald, 22)

Asking God to reveal His plan for me through life's circumstances and being willing to do what is revealed is the first step in discovering it. Following His leading may not be easy, but it is the essential step to inner satisfaction and peace.

God's will encompasses every aspect of what one should be doing, but it is certain that uppermost in His desire is our working to make better whatever situation we find ourselves in. The divine energies expend themselves most efficiently in the lives of those who take as their uppermost purpose the glorifying of God in the tasks of each new day. "From of old no one has heard or perceived by the ear, no eye has seen a God besides thee, who works for those who wait for him. Thou meetest him that joyfully works righteousness, those that remember thee in thy ways" (Isa. 64:4, 5).

I think it true for all of us that eternity will reveal how much greater good could have been accomplished if yet more careful attention had been given along the way to the further good God really wanted us to do. "We know that in everything God works for good with those who love him" (Rom 8:28). His plan is the only one worth working. Humbly placing oneself to work at God's disposal issues in the creation of true righteousness, effects true accomplishment here, and ensures happiness hereafter.

CHAPTER THREE
PROBLEMS WITH PATHS

In the garden, as in life, thought must first be given to the paths. Paths determine perspective. A large part of the reason for making a flower bed is how it will look when done, and the look is determined by the angles of view. It is from the vantage point of the paths that the garden will be viewed and enjoyed. So I decided where I wanted people to walk for the best effect and laid out paths accordingly. Gentle curves are the rule, not too abrupt or too many. Long straight paths without a view of a curve or some focal interest at the end should be avoided.

The next step is to imagine various plants in relation to that path. Planning is fun. All sorts of possibilities soon present themselves to the imagination. In general, one should envision low creeping or arching plants, such as alyssum or petunias, placed along the paths, with the heights of other plants rising somewhat irregularly toward points of focus farther away. However, if the bed is along a larger patio or driveway, consider having a strip of lawn between it and the flower bed.

Since working with plants requires being near them—sometimes frequently—during the season, it is handiest if the beds along the path are not too wide for the gardener to reach the plants farthest from the edges. In the case of larger, wider beds, however, one should plan to place stepping stones where needed. These should be comparatively small in relation to the size of the main path and unobtrusively placed. Ideally, plant growth should almost hide them, but not completely. Any other paths that are needed should be pleasingly proportioned to the size of the garden beds and wide enough for comfortable strolling; three foot is a good minimum width.

Choosing the materials to construct the path can be perplexing. Often the deciding factor is how much money one chooses to spend. Very attractive paths can be made from slabs of limestone—what people at the quarry call "steppers"—that are available in various shades and styles. Remove four or five inches of dirt, lay a strip of plastic to keep weeds from growing, add an inch or so of sand or stone siftings (of which any quarry has an abundance), and then place the steppers in close relation one to another, keeping the sides of the path as straight as possible. Fill in between the stones with limestone siftings. Creeping thyme planted-not too frequently-in the cracks is attractive, provided one keeps the plants from creeping all over the place. Stepped on, the sprigs of thyme emit a pleasing odor.

We chose more economical material, however, which also works very well: wood chips. Chips are often easily obtained. Since we had an arborist take down several undesirable trees for us, we had a large supply at hand. Tree services must dispose of their loads of chips somewhere, and if working near by, they may even bring them to you gratis. If the chips are distributed thickly enough—three or four inches deep—weeds will not grow through for at least a year. And when they begin to do so, spot spraying with vegetation killer quickly removes them. A thin layer of fresh wood chips may be added about every third year, as they do decompose in time.

Robert Frost knew that paths were a vital part of a pleasing garden, and he also had a keen eye for the analogy that garden paths suggest. In "God's Garden" he wrote:

God made a beauteous garden
  With lovely flowers strown,
But one straight, narrow pathway
  That was not overgrown.
And to this beauteous garden
  He brought mankind to live,
And said: "To you, my children,
  These lovely flowers I give.
Prune ye my vines and fig trees,
  With care my flowerets tend,
But keep the pathway open,
  Your home is at the end."
Then came another master,
  Who did not love mankind,
And planted on the pathway
  Gold flowers for them to find.
And mankind saw the bright flowers,
  That, glitt'ring in the sun,
Quite hid the thorns of av'rice
  That poison blood and bone;
And far off many wandered,
  And when life's night came on,
They still were seeking gold flowers,
  Lost, helpless, and alone.
O, cease to heed the glamour
  That blinds your foolish eyes,
Look upward to the glitter
  Of stars in God's clear skies.
Their ways are pure and harmless

> And will not lead astray,
> But aid your erring footsteps
>   To keep the narrow way.
> And when the sun shines brightly
>   Tend flowers that God has given
> And keep the pathway open
>   That leads you on to heaven.
> (*Complete Poems, Prose, & Plays*, 503)

Living one's life is a good deal like following a path, and the Bible often uses that analogy. The pathway in Eden that Frost imagines answers to the Narrow Way spoken of in the Sermon on the Mount. Christ advised his followers to enter by it, "for the gate is wide and the way is easy that leads to destruction, and those who enter by it are many. For the gate is narrow, and the way is hard, that leads to life, and those who find it are few" (Matt. 7:13, 14). These are among the most sobering words our Lord spoke.

Deciding which path one takes through life is the primary decision a person makes. To give the decision no thought, as the "many" do, and simply follow one's inclinations, letting happen what happens, is inevitably to walk the Broad Way whose end is destruction. Christ's words are awesome, and they are not quoted nearly often enough.

Like the pathway through a garden, once one is on the Narrow Way all of life is viewed in relation to it. The Way provides the perspective by which every other thing in life is valued and properly appreciated. Furthermore, the traveler faces an entire set of concerns and challenges that people traveling the Broad Way know nothing of. In John Bunyan's *The Pilgrim's Progress*, all Christian's experiences upon the Way are occasioned by his having chosen to be Christian; none but those few who have made a similar commitment understand him. But Christian discovers the singular path he has chosen opens upon a liberating life that offers strength for his trials, peace for his heart, and the joy of finding his true home at the end.

Here is a profound paradox. Contrary to popular belief, the Narrow Way of the true believer is not a confining one. It is the complete opposite of the paths of unrighteousness, ways that are really narrow in the worst sense of that word. It is the Broad Way that demands conformity to the fads and fashions of popular culture. Walking the Broad Way ushers in the frightening sameness of the lives of promiscuous people with their spiritually destructive practices. Its so-called broadness is an illusion, all its enticing promises notwithstanding, for it robs one of true individuality and leads to misery, both here and hereafter. George MacDonald mused on the real narrowness of popular ways and the basic loveliness of the true:

> The narrow ways trodden of men are miserable;
> they have high walls on each side, and but an
> occasional glimpse of the sky above. . . . The true
> way, though narrow, is not unlovely; most footpaths
> are lovelier than high-roads. It may be full of toil, but
> it cannot be miserable. It has not walls, but fields
> and forests and gardens around it, and limitless sky
> overhead. It has its sorrows, but many of them lie only
> on its borders, and they that leave the path gather them
> (*Donal Grant*, 128).

Discerning just where the Narrow Way lies through the thicket of specific situations in one's life is often difficult. It is the way of upright living, the "path of righteousness" in which David said the Lord leads "for his name's sake" (Psa. 23:3) and testified, "Thou dost show me the path of life" (Psa. 16:11). The way the Lord leads a person is related to one's own circumstances, personality traits, and opportunities. It always consists simply of doing the right thing—which is the will of God—in whatever situation one finds oneself.

"Trust in the Lord with all your heart, and do not rely on your own insight. In all your ways acknowledge him, and he will make straight your paths" (Prov. 3:5, 6). One's home is at the end. In my experience, the still small voice that directs attention to just where the right path lies may most often be heard amid the peace and solitude that working in the garden affords.

CHAPTER FOUR
LET IT BE

I have never planned a flower bed that did not in fact turn out differently from what I had intended. I have tried to imagine vividly what I wanted, calculated accurate measurements of the garden site, transferred them to drafting paper, and pasted colorful pictures clipped from nursery catalogs on duplicate sheets. (It is a pleasant way to pass dreary winter afternoons.) In the summer, however, after the plans have been carefully executed and the plants are all performing, the bed I look upon has a reality of its own, quite distinct from what I had thought it would be in the planning stage.

Admittedly, the bed is certainly better than if no plans had been made, but its reality falls short of my expectations. What to do? I can have one of two responses: I can be dissatisfied and nurse my disappointment, or I can reconcile myself to reality and enjoy what is before me. The latter response is the only sensible one; and when I make it, I find my pleasure in the mystery of gardening is deepened. To be dissatisfied is not only to waste another season but also to nurture the dangerous exercise of preferring the images resident in the mind to the real flowers before me.

To be a gardener is to be a partner with nature, and nature seems to delight in doing the unexpected. Granted, some of the surprises can be unsettling: the aster whose bloom I had so much anticipated has fallen prey to blight; the delphinium is not the color the nursery tag promised it to be. But when the wilted aster is removed, neighboring plants soon fill the empty space, and the delphinium, a lovely pink with a white eye, offers an unexpected pleasure, even though it does alter the color scheme I had in mind. It is, in fact, really lovely. I never fail to marvel how so many colors in nature have a way of achieving a pleasing blend, in defiance of the logic of the color wheel. Or so it seems to me. Wisdom lies in carefully planning a bed as the necessary first step, but, after one has done one's best, greater wisdom lies in reconciling oneself to what actually happens.

And so it is with all of life. Coventry Patmore very wisely wrote:

> Leave the *form* of the future wholly to Him; not in anything insisting on your natural desires, which, if you attain to life, will all, indeed, be fulfilled beyond desire, though perhaps in modes the very reverse of those you expect and desire now. You do not truly "love God and keep His commandments" by insisting, in desire, upon anything, even the salvation of your dearest and nearest. If you believe in and love God, you will effectually believe that He loves all who are capable of His love far better than you do, and you will be heartily sure that you will give, when you know all, a joyful consent to decrees which may seem to you now most hard and terrible. (*The Rod, The Root and The Flower*, 168)

The discipline of committing something entirely to God and patiently waiting before Him for its resolution is one of the most difficult of the Christian life. One should do all one feels led to do, as though everything depended upon one's own efforts, yet at the same time commit in prayer the situation entirely to God, trusting as though everything depended upon His resolutions, as indeed it does. Then, be entirely satisfied with what comes to pass.

The earnest Christian who observes the Lord's workings soon learns that God's thoughts and ways transcend and trump one's own. "For my thoughts are not your thoughts, neither are your ways my ways, says the Lord. For as the heavens are higher than the earth, so are my ways higher than your ways and my thoughts than your thoughts" (Isa. 55:8, 9). Often, one feels intensely that the solution to a particular problem is obvious. If God would follow our advice all would be as it should be. But events seldom happen as we think they should, all our prayers notwithstanding. Wisdom lies in seeing what God is indeed doing and attempting to work with him, acquiescing in what is. Our Lord said, "My food is to do the will of him who sent me, and to accomplish his work" (John 4:34). James assures us "The prayer of a righteous man has great power in its effects" (James 5:16). It remains for eternity to reveal the full nature of those effects.

CHAPTER FIVE

WHAT ABOUT TILTH?

To be successful, a gardener must have good soil with which to work. The best soil consists of various solid particles with ample organic matter through which air and water can readily pass. It is home to a teeming population of minute forms of life—microorganisms—which are vital to plant growth. It contains considerable humus—a dark, airy substance derived from well-decomposed organic materials, such as leaves and decayed plants.

Compacted clay soil is an utter disaster for gardening, as is blow sand. However, many suburbanites must deal with an impervious clay. To achieve a firm and level surface upon which to build, developers tend to begin by removing the top soil and leaving the hard clay subsoil upon which to work. Lawns can be fairly successfully grown by returning a thin layer of good soil and unrolling sod over such a substructure, but gardening demands a much deeper layer of top soil, and the subsoil must allow ready drainage. Whatever it takes to achieve a bed of at least six inches of well drained organically rich growing medium that drains nicely must be done.

Good top soil can be trucked in. The ideal is to achieve the airy consistency known as good tilth, so that roots can more easily establish themselves and water drain quickly away. If you order soil trucked in, be certain you are purchasing soil that is in good tilth, not simply black clay. Pulverized clay may appear satisfactory, but it will soon revert to its solid state. Insist on loam. Add to it sufficient soil conditioners to achieve a light, fluffy consistency, so that you can run your hands through it easily. Peat moss, perlite or vermiculite, composted manure, and leaf mold are all good, a balanced mixture of these additives being ideal. Fallen leaves tilled into a bed in the fall will decompose over the winter and do much toward achieving the ideal consistency.

The best way to attain good tilth is to till in compost each year, but when one is getting started on a new plot, compost has probably not yet been made.

For immediate use, peat moss (buy Canadian brown) is very good. Commercial vermiculite and perlite are good to ensure drainage and at the same time help make moisture available to plant roots. A moderate amount of dehydrated manure effectively adds plant nutrients. Be wary, however, of adding fresh manure, as it is "hot" and will very likely burn your plants. The so-called composted manure that is sold in bags in garden centers is generally simply barnyard dirt, all right in itself but a rather expensive additive.

Unless one achieves good drainage, all other efforts are in vain. To determine drainage, dig a hole a foot or so deep and fill it with water. If the water takes more than an hour to soak away, drastic steps must be taken to hasten drainage. If the problem is a heavy clay subsoil, liberally applying gypsum may help. If the entire area is low, receiving run-off water, building beds raised above ground level may be the answer. That requires purchasing two-inch planks of at least eight inches in width—of whatever length needed— and staking them in upright patterns no more than five feet apart, so that one can handily reach the middle. But if the area you are working has formerly sustained a good turf, chances are that with a little help it will grow good vegetables and flowers.

While all this work can be done in early spring, accomplishing it in the fall is preferable, because the reconditioned soil allowed to overwinter reestablishes its own organic balance as the various components and bacteria reposition themselves. Melting snows soak gently into it, depositing moisture and nitrogen. To proceed directly to planting without careful preparation is certain to result in a disappointing effect.

Christ used the metaphor of different types of soil and seed to illustrate the range of responses people make to divine truth. He said the Word of God is like seed planted in the heart. Just as any seed needs good soil in which to sprout and grow, so a person must be open and receptive in his innermost being to what God is saying. The Bible speaks directly to the heart. Unreceptive attitudes are like bad soil—compacted clay or blow sand—that prevents proper germination. The widespread enmity to the simple Gospel message is one of the great mysteries of the human heart. George MacDonald mused:

> Why is it that men and women will welcome any tale of love, devotion, and sacrifice from one to another of themselves, but turn from the least hint at the existence of a perfect love at the root of it all? With such a message to them, a man is maundering prophet! Is it not that their natures are yet so far from the ideal, the natural, the true, that the words

of the prophet rouse in them no vision, no poorest perception of spiritual fact? (*Weighed and Wanting*, 23)

A spirit of unwillingness to receive the plain sense of the Word of God is a sure indicator of how deep and pervading human fallenness is, and, of course, makes it the easier for the evil one to snatch the truth away. What should be more directly alarming to the professing believer is the warning concerning all that prevents spiritual development and personal growth. Distracting concerns are like weeds that choke the desired plants, our Lord said, the worst of which are "the cares of the world and the delight in riches."

It is easy for the person who has heard many sermons on the Parable of the Sower to see it as being a purely evangelistic text. It applies to first-time hearers, not to me. Think again. The Word is to be received continually with childlike openness. While the first truths the heart received are like older plants growing and maturing, truths more recently encountered are like plants just germinating, that require careful tending. The admonition, "Today, when you hear his voice, do not harden your heart. . ." (Heb. 3:15), applies to us all.

CHAPTER SIX
SEEDS GROW, BUT WHO KNOWS HOW?

Once planned and prepared, beds must be filled with plants. The number of plants required to fill a bed of any size can quickly become very costly. I greatly prefer growing my own plants to buying them. Much of the fun of gardening resides in patiently helping and watching plants grow, from germination through to fruit or flower.

What miracle, what mystery matches that of a germinating seed? Often a seed is no larger than a tiny speck, so that making any kind of orderly distribution in planting is a real challenge. Yet under the right conditions the stalk, and cotyledons (or the first set of leaves) spring up, then leaves and branches, blossoms, buds, flowers and fruit. God delights in continual creation. Those who see the seemingly endless repetitions of nature as the product of impersonal natural law instead of the miraculous creating power of God pull blinders over their own eyes that obliterate the wonder they should be experiencing. G.K. Chesterton puts it well:

> ... it might be true that the sun rises regularly because he never gets tired of rising. His routine might be due, not to a lifelessness, but to a rush of life. The thing I mean can be seen, for instance, in children, when they find some game or joke that they specially enjoy. A child kicks his legs rhythmically through excess, not absence, of life. Because children have abounding vitality, because they are in spirit fierce and free, therefore they want things repeated and unchanged. They always say, "Do it again"; and the grown-up person does it again until he is nearly dead. For grown-up people are not strong enough to exult in monotony. But perhaps God is strong enough to exult in monotony. It is possible that God says every morning, "Do it again" to the sun; and every evening, "Do it again" to the moon. It may not be automatic necessity that makes all daisies alike; it may be that God makes every daisy separately, but has never got tired of making them. It may be that he has the eternal appetite of infancy; for we have sinned and grown old, and our Father is younger than we. (*Orthodoxy*, 108-109.)

The constant repetitions, the rhythms of the universe, the mighty urge of life to grow and flower, are, if one but gives it thought, endless sources of wonder. The rhythms of day after day, month after month through all our years provide a context for the ceaseless rhythms of new life and growth. The process never loses its capacity to marvel and delight anyone who pays the slightest attention. What a potential resides in a seed!

A gardener finds delight in being a partner in the process. It is difficult to wait for the frost-free days of spring to begin planting. The growing season can be nicely lengthened by beginning the process in late winter—inside. The rewards of beginning early are many, and not much equipment is needed. Starting plants indoors enables a person to do more precise planning for the season ahead, makes for much earlier summer blooms, thereby extending the enjoyment of the season, and is much cheaper than buying plants at the nursery later on.

To get started, I build some simple racks in the basement from two-by-fours and sheets of one-half inch plywood, mounting fluorescent light fixtures on chains above the shelves so that the lights can be raised as the little plants grow. With the two-by-fours placed upright from joists to floor I have ample room for three shelves on each rack. For more modest undertakings, one needs at least one fluorescent light fixture with two fresh cool white tubes (special "grow lights" are expensive and really unnecessary), a bag of sterile germinating mixture, some small sterile trays, and, of course, seeds. Sterility is essential to keep the seedlings from falling prey to various fungi that will quickly kill them all. In the trade it is called "dampening off."

The germinating medium, which is available in little bags at any garden center, needs first to be wetted and kneaded. I am careful not to use more water initially than is necessary to make a smooth seed bed, putting the wetted medium into three-by-five-inch or four-by-six-inch plastic trays and then indenting rows in them with the aid of a small stick the same length as the tray.

Different seeds have different planting requirements; directions for planting are upon most seed packets. Some seeds are so minute that it is a good idea to purchase a little plastic planting device available at garden centers; one can also mix a little fine sand with the seeds and distribute the mixture. Gently press the seeds into the soil. I plant fairly thickly, as the little plants will be transplanted as soon as they have grown two healthy sets of leaves beyond the cotyledons. Comparative ease in transplanting is the only factor to consider in spacing the seeds. Most seeds must be slightly covered, some not, as they need light for germination. Seed packages contain instructions. The medium itself can be used for covering, but fine vermiculite works well.

After the tray is planted, place it in a larger tray of tepid water for a few minutes, allowing the medium to absorb water from the bottom. Then cover the seed tray with plastic wrap to keep humidity high and place it two or three inches under a fluorescent light fixture. Lay a piece of light cardboard on top if the particular seeds you are working with—such as pansies—need darkness for germination. Instructions on the packet will alert you to this need. If they do, be sure to check in three or four days, and each day thereafter, removing the cardboard as soon as you see the slightest sign of germination. Otherwise, the emerging plants will quickly reach for light, becoming hopelessly spindly, and all is lost.

CHAPTER SEVEN
GIVE UP AND GIVE OVER

What a fascinating reality growth is! A person cannot see it happening, nor hear it (although I remember as a child being by a cornfield on hot, humid nights and hearing the corn stalks pop). If I rivet my attention upon a plant, watching it day after day, it seems static, perhaps a cause for worry. Yet when I leave it for only two or three days and return, I can note the changes taking place. And how satisfying it is to see spurts of the longed for development after a good rain on a hot summer's day!

All I as a gardener can do is to create the optimal conditions under which growth can take place. I cannot myself make it happen. I am utterly dependent upon the mystery fulfilling itself again each season. My role, beyond the cultivating and nurturing, is to watch it with joy and satisfaction. I am satisfied with its various stages only because I see them as the necessary preliminaries to the final product. They are never ends in themselves.

Growth is indispensable to healthy life. Everything in nature is either growing or decaying. "The force that through the green fuse drives the flower / Drives my green age; that blasts the roots of trees / Is my destroyer," Dylan Thomas wrote (*Collected Poems of Dylan Thomas*, 10). Development, maturity, and death. But death is the prelude to new life. "In my end is my beginning" ("East Coker," *Complete Poems and Plays*, 129). Demise precedes renewal through the seed, and the mysterious cycle continues. Christ saw in the natural cycle the pattern that is indispensable to true life, the life eternal. "Truly, truly, I say to you, unless a grain of wheat falls into the earth and dies, it remains alone; but if it dies, it bears much fruit" (John 12:24).

Much can be learned from the metaphor. A gardener must be a person of faith, persistence, patience, and confidence: faith in the mystery of life, the incredible fact that a tiny seed in dying will produce, step by step, plant and bud and fruit; patience and persistence in the cultivating and nurturing process; and confidence that, the right conditions prevailing, the expected end will be realized, bringing with it the satisfaction and joy that belongs to the husbandman.

Just as, after I have done my duty with a plant, it is foolish for me to stand over it day after day, fretting about its welfare, so it is foolish for me to fret about my growth as a Christian. After I have done my part, I must let the Lord do His, and allow him the necessary time for maturation to take place. My part, to be sure, must be wholly fulfilled: Complete commitment to Christ, renewed each morning. The seed of eternal life is thereby nourished and begins to thrive in good soil. Nothing short of complete surrender will do: giving up and giving over. This biblical prescription is directly opposed to that of striving on my own to be what I know the Bible requires of me. That leads to failure, of one kind or another. Even though I may through strength of will momentarily achieve what passes for virtue in this situation or that, the result is pride, the chief of sins.

But once I have given myself completely to Christ, Christ's life is within, and living becomes the adventure of faith He intends it to be. My life has become Christ's, along with all its problems, inadequacies, and shortcomings. Christ must be left to deal with them, and deal with them He will. My part is to provide and maintain the right conditions for optimum growth— letting my spirit feed upon Biblical truths, being faithful in meeting with fellow Christians in worship and fellowship, always keeping in mind I am Christ's representative in each day's situations. The inevitable failures are quickly confessed, and in simple sincerity

I try again. "There is therefore now no condemnation for those who are in Christ Jesus" (Rom 8:1). If God does not condemn the sincere Christian, neither should we condemn ourselves.

I may at times be filled with unrest and dissatisfaction with the distance I stand from the perfection to which I am called as a follower of Christ. ("You, therefore, must be perfect, as your heavenly Father is perfect" Matt. 5:48.) The tone of contemporary American culture exacerbates this feeling with its emphasis upon instant success. People at large are worshiping the great god Efficiency. We must have results here and now. Corporations must be "lean and mean," cutthroat competition demands the quickest performance at the least cost. One effect of this attitude in our daily lives is a constant effort to compress time. We demand instant coffee, instant meals, instant gratifications. Our cell phones give us instant communication with whomever. And, in the Christian life, we want instant maturity.

Not only is such expectation unreal, it is a serious misplacement of concern. The Christian is asked to love God, love his neighbor, and forget the self. We are not to fret over ourselves because we do not seem to grow; we are rather to realize it is God's work within, and provide as much as we are able, the conditions for it to take place. Simone Weil gives provocative expression to the process:

Over the infinity of space and time, the infinitely more infinite love of God comes to possess us. He comes at his own time. We have the power to consent to receive him or to refuse. If we remain deaf, he comes back again and again like a beggar, but also, like a beggar, one day he stops coming. If we consent, God puts a little seed in us and he goes away again. . . . On the whole . . . the seed grows of itself. A day comes when the soul belongs to God, when it not only consents to love but when truly and effectively it loves. Then in its turn it must cross the universe to go to God. The soul does not love like a creature with created love. The love within it is divine, uncreated; for it is the love of God for God that is passing through it. God alone is capable of loving God. We can only consent to give up our own feelings so as to allow free passage in our soul for this love. That is the meaning of denying oneself. We are created for this consent, and for this alone.

Divine Love crossed the infinity of space and time to come from God to us. But how can it repeat the journey in the opposite direction, starting from a finite creature? When the seed of divine love placed in us has grown and become a tree, how can we, we who bear it, take it back to its origin? . . . .It seems impossible, but there is a way-a way with which we are familiar. We know quite well in what likeness this tree is made, this tree that has grown within us, this most beautiful tree where the birds of the air come and perch. . . . It was the seed of this tree that God placed within us, without our knowing what seed it was.... In a dimension that does not belong to space, that is not time, that is indeed quite a different dimension.... the soul, without leaving the place and the instant where the body to which it is united is situated, can cross the totality of space and time and come into the very presence of God. ...Saint Paul was perhaps thinking about things of this kind when he said: "That ye, being rooted and grounded in love, may be able to comprehend with all saints what is the breadth, and length, and depth, and height; and to know the love of Christ, which passeth knowledge." (*Waiting for God*, 79-82)

God means for the Christian life to be a joyous adventure, not a fretting over failures. Obedience gradually becomes easier; growth does occur. The growth is His part, not ours. It occurs, not by effort, but by consent.

CHAPTER EIGHT

NATURE IS NEVER SPENT

It is impossible to put into words the glory one encounters when observing nature at its best. Language fails; the most brilliant of metaphors only convey a glimpse of the truth. Such is the character of spring. The swelling of buds; the sudden appearance of crocuses, daffodils, and tulips unfolding their glory; the inimitable green of April's grass speak not only of the awakening of life on every hand but of the promise, the joy, that is in life itself.

Some people, however, refuse to allow even the most breathtaking of scenes to give them joy. They say the pity is the beauty will not last. Robert Frost, in contemplating a crocus, captures the mood:

> *Nature's first green is gold,*
> *Her hardest hue to hold.*
> *Her early leaf's a flower;*
> *But only so an hour.*
> *Then leaf subsides to leaf.*
> *So Eden sank to grief,*
> *So dawn goes down to day.*
> *Nothing gold can stay.*
> (Complete Poems, Prose, & Plays, 206)

This is the voice of the "realist," the voice of common sense, and its basic truth is surely not to be denied. That such falling off is inevitable, however, must not prevent a person from fully savoring the beauty of nature, exulting in the joy one feels. Even the realization that all beauty fades enhances the present perception. Were it not so, beauty would lose its appeal. Wallace Stevens was right when he observed, "Death is the mother of beauty," (*Collected Poems of Wallace Stevens*, 68) although the conclusions he drew from the principle are so pathetically wrong. Beauty, because it is fleeting, not only intensifies the Christian's enjoyment of the present moment but also strengthens hope.

Scripture suggests that the beauty we encounter now offers but a taste of that which God has in store for His faithful ones in the world to come. David felt such a foretaste when he cried:

> The heavens are telling the glory of God; and the firmament proclaims his handiwork. Day to day pours forth speech, and night to night declares knowledge. There is no speech, nor are there words; their voice is not heard; yet their voice goes out through all the earth, and their words to the end of the world. (Psa. 19:1-4)

Paul, looking into the future, saw a "great weight of glory" that will one day be experienced by all who live by the unseen rather than the seen. At no season does the glory of God speak so loudly through nature as in spring. The very fact that all the promises of spring are not fulfilled in the seasons that follow suggests this world is not our true home, that those who allow their lives to be renewed in God shall one day realize the glory that nature faintly promises in its springtime of gladness.

Not only so, but the dynamic of springtime life witnesses how persistently and strongly nature opposes and triumphs over the destructive forces of decay and death that beset her, as well as the corruptions that society heaps upon her. Everywhere new life is triumphing over death. Leo Tolstoy expresses the thought in the opening of his novel *Resurrection*. He introduces his reader to the coming of spring in a Russian town:

> Though hundreds of thousands had done their very best to disfigure the small piece of land on which they were crowded together: paving the ground with stones, scraping away every vestige of vegetation, cutting down the trees, turning away birds and beasts, filling the air with the smoke of naphtha and coal—still spring was spring, even in the town.
>
> The sun shone warm, the air was balmy, the grass, where it did not get scraped away, revived and sprang up everywhere: between the paving-stones as well as on the narrow strips of lawn on the boulevards. The birches, the poplars, and the wild cherry trees were unfolding their gummy and fragrant leaves, the bursting buds were swelling on the lime trees; crows, sparrows, and pigeons, filled with the joy of spring, were getting their nests ready; the flies were buzzing along the walls warmed by the sunshine. All were glad: the plants, the birds, the insects, and the children. But men, grown-up men and women, did not leave off cheating and tormenting themselves and each other. It was not this spring morning men thought sacred and worthy of consideration, not the beauty of God's world, given for a joy to all creatures—the beauty which inclines the heart to peace, to harmony, and to love—but only their own devices for enslaving one another.
>
> Thus, in the prison office of the Government town . . .(*Resurrection*, 19)

—and the story is launched. In the experiences of his

hero, Tolstoy narrates the struggle of undertaking to live an upright moral and spiritual life among such people. His vision is perennially true. People who are oblivious to the natural beauty surrounding them choose rather to imprison themselves in self-centered attitudes and apply their energies solely to personal advancement with no thought to the harmful effects upon others. The terrible result is the spiritual diminishment of themselves.

Although every present expression of beauty fades, the energies in nature that engender it and make for growth and becoming never cease. Nature never gives up; its impulses never flag. In a sonnet of praise, Gerard Manley Hopkins gives memorable expression to the truth:

> *The world is charged with the grandeur of God.*
>   *It will flame out, like shining from shook foil;*
>   *It gathers to a greatness, like the ooze of oil*
> *Crushed. Why do men then now not reck his rod?*
> *Generations have trod, have trod, have trod;*
>   *And all is seared with trade; bleared, smeared with toil;*
>   *And wears man's smudge and shares man's smell: the soil*
> *Is bare now, nor can foot feel, being shod.*
>
> *And for all this, nature is never spent;*
>   *There lives the dearest freshness deep down things,*
> *And though the last lights off the black West went*

> *Oh, morning, at the brown brink eastward, springs–*
> Because the Holy Ghost over the bent
>   World broods with warm breast and with ah! bright wings.
>
> (The Poems of Gerald Manley Hopkins, 66)

The true life in nature is the presence of the Holy Spirit bringing the energies of grace to birth, energies that reside even in the bentness of things, just as a dove broods upon its eggs to hatch them. A person can live in harmony with such energies or not, as one chooses, but the grace of God knows no cessation, and He is beckoning those who love Him toward "what no eye has seen, nor ear heard, nor the heart of man conceived" (1 Cor. 2:9). Spring, I think, contains a foretaste of what He has prepared.

CHAPTER NINE
WHY NOT SIMPLY PULL IT OUT?

A beautiful garden is a clean one. No weeds. Working with virgin soil, as I have been on our lot, means wrestling with particular varieties of weeds that have established themselves over many years. Garlic mustard, for instance, plagues me everywhere. Burdock, too, in select patches. Creeping ivy has taken over some areas, choking out all else, and wild violets pervade the lawn. The quickest way of ridding oneself of entire colonies is to apply a chemical herbicide, available at any garden center. If a person is determined to be an organic gardener, vinegar will do the job. Within a couple weeks the whole area is barren.

Removing weeds, and keeping them out, is perhaps the gardener's most time-consuming task. But the satisfaction and pride one feels when the task is done is itself adequate compensation for the energy expended. Like any other of the tasks in the garden, one should enjoy—or at least not mind—doing it, or else quit aspiring to a nice garden.

One of the curious things about weeds is that a person wants to know them by name. I am at a loss to know why, when I learned that the name of the ubiquitous growth on my lot was garlic mustard, I felt more in control of it. Each spring it appears anew, but at least I know who my enemy is and can learn about it in literature on weeds and feel some power over it.

No gardener needs to be told that weeds are certain to appear in any garden. An abundance of seeds is in any soil, waiting with seemingly infinite patience for the right conditions to germinate. They are more various than birds of the air, with new and strange specimens regularly appearing. Chemicals are now on the market that will kill a weed with a squirt, but, once desirable plants are planted, it is wretchedly difficult to keep the residue of the spray from affecting them, making that approach less practical than it sounds. It takes a considerable amount of time and effort, and the results are not immediate. Why not simply kneel down and pull the weed? Or use that most basic of all gardening tools, the hoe?

The traditional approach is less complicated and more immediate. Unless one is working with a larger area and wants all the vegetation killed, the old way of pulling and hoeing is simpler and quicker. Yes, in another couple weeks more unwanted growth may be appearing, but don't give up. Consistent and patient eradication will greatly reduce the new sprouts that, like the poor, are always with us.

The best approach to dealing with weeds is to eliminate them from garden beds in the spring as early as they appear. The beds are much easier to keep clean thereafter. Weeds are removed rather easily then, as the soil tends to be moist and rather loose. To wait until the weeds develop strong root systems and the ground is drier makes the task much harder. An overgrown bed can not only be an insurmountable task to clean, but also the true garden plants have been made to suffer, perhaps have even been overwhelmed and choked to death.

Weeds, which are simply unwanted plants, offer an apt metaphor for all the unwanted thoughts and attitudes in the mind, all those one really wishes were not there but seems helpless to eradicate. As the presence of weeds in my garden embarrasses me, so do unbecoming thoughts and acts in my mind make me ashamed of myself and detract from my living a happy and truly enjoyable life. To dismiss them is like eradicating weeds. Milton's Adam was right when before the fall he instructed Eve, "Evil into the mind of God or Man / May come and go, so unapprov'd, and leave / No spot or blame behind" ("Paradise Lost", *Complete Poems and Major Prose*, 305). It is when the will capitulates and entertains the foul thought that we become culpable. Like Goethe's Faust, one must not say the fatal words "Abide, thou art so fair." Turning one's attention to something else is a good way of escape.

E.A. Robinson aptly uses the metaphor of a garden overrun with weeds to depict a wasted life:

> *There is a fenceless garden overgrown*
> *With buds and blossoms*
> *and all sorts of leaves;*
> *And once, among the roses and the sheaves,*
> *The Gardener and I were there alone.*
> *He led me to the plot where I had thrown*
> *The fennel of my days on wasted ground,*
> *And in that riot of sad weeds I found*
> *The fruitage of a life that was my own.*
> (*Collected Poems*, 86)

How easy it is to allow one's life to be like an untended garden, overrun with weeds. Just as any plot of ground, left to itself, becomes overwhelmed with rank and ugly growth, so does the human heart. Left to itself, it becomes foul. Talents are undeveloped, time is squandered. Unless remedied, a life is ruined, and aching remorse and maddening regret will beset a person throughout eternity. But the remedy is near at hand. It lies with God, not one's self.

One cannot say too strongly that it is by the grace of God alone, and not by individual effort, that the human heart is weeded. I must, of course, first want my own weeds removed, but I am entirely unable to do it on my own. The roots are far too deeply embedded, the growth too rank, the heart itself as impervious as stone. I must fully cooperate with the process, but it is the Spirit of God alone that is able to effect the eternal difference.

As with weeds, so with sins: one must begin by fully recognizing and acknowledging them. Take stock honestly and name them accurately before God. Some have sat before a mirror and addressed the self image there with a full naming of all that one knows ought not to be present in the life. Tell God you want them utterly removed. Simply receive Him at his word and believe that He will deal with them. "If we confess our sins, he is faithful and just, and will forgive our sins and cleanse us from all unrighteousness" (1 John 1:9).

Then, try being occupied with what makes for the heart's true and healthy growth. ". . .whatever is true, whatever is honorable, whatever is just, whatever is pure, whatever is lovely, whatever is gracious, if there is any excellence, if there is anything worthy of praise, think about these things" (Phil 4:8). Life is filled with all of these, although they are often not readily apparent. Developing the habit of discerning what is good in life reveals where the grace of God is practicing "steadfast love, justice, and righteousness in the earth; for in these things I delight, says the Lord" (Jer. 9:24). Weeds have a way of continually germinating, but root them out early, and work with the Gardener to develop the fruit He prizes.

CHAPTER TEN
A SMILE ON ALL CREATION

Incredible as it may seem to the average person, I cannot but see the plants I nurture and cultivate as in some sense having personalities. No one can deny they are living entities, and some experimenters contend that plants experience emotions that can be gauged. However that may be, they are living, growing things purposefully developing toward the yielding of flower or fruit. Like people the world over, each plant is individual and distinct from all others in its species, a very specific being.

Each plant and I must work together if its potential is to be fully realized. Depending upon the variety, my role as gardener is smaller or larger, but I do have a part in helping each one to perform its best. Whether or not I work correctly with a given plant makes an immense difference in the flowers that plant will produce. This is one of the reasons why I love the dahlia more than any other flower, for caring properly for it at appropriate times throughout the growing season makes an enormous difference in the blooms the plant produces. Correct fertilization, disbranching and disbudding at the right times, watching for and dealing with insects and fungi before the damage is done, all make a large contribution toward prize-winning blooms.

Just as plants in my garden "do their own thing," fulfilling what they in their intrinsic characters are, yet are utterly dependent upon a gardener's knowledge and proper attention, so is the believer in the garden of God. "But I am like a green olive tree in the house of God," David writes. "I trust in the steadfast love of God for ever and ever. I will thank thee for ever, because thou hast done it" (Psa. 52:8,9). Dante makes compelling use of a similar metaphor in *The Divine Comedy*. After he has traversed hell and purgatory and nears the topmost region of heaven, he is met by St. John, who questions him about the reality of his love. John asks whether it is simply rhetorical statement or if it has been effectively expressed in his life. Dante, now strong in faith, replies first by listing four fundamental realities that bind him to God. They are, as it were, contributions that God, the Gardener of souls, has provided him. Dante then closes with a moving metaphor likening the world to a garden dependent upon the skills of the Great Gardener:

> *The being of the world and my own state,*
> *The death He died that I might live the more,*
> *The hope in which I, by faith, participate,*
> *The living truth which I conveyed before,*
> *Have dredged me from the sea of wrongful love,*
> *And of the right have set me on the shore.*
> *And through the garden of the world I rove,*
> *Enamoured of its leaves in measure solely*
> *As God the Gardener nurtures them above.*
> (The Comedy of Dante Alighieri: Paradise, 284)

Because Dante has learned to see the entire world as a garden God is growing, he is able to move through it with relaxed delight, confident in the knowledge and expertise of the One who is working toward an abundant harvest. Because he knows that God's care for His creation is steadfast in its purpose and complete in its wisdom, he discerns a smile on all created things and exults:

And all I saw, meseemed to see therein
A smile of all creation; thus through eye
And ear I drew the inebriate rapture in.

O joy no tongue can tell! O ecstasy!
　O perfect life fulfilled of love and peace!
　　O wealth past want, that ne'er shall fade nor fly!
(Ibid., 91)

It is after the redeemed poet has come to understand fully God's meaning and purpose in his universe and has had his own spirit brought into full harmony with them that he sees a smile on all creation and breathes pure joy. It is not in the nature of the Christian life to walk constantly in such transport of delight, but the obedient Christian nevertheless occasionally catches, by the grace of God, glimpses of a fulfillment too grand for words and knows moments of such realization and praise, a consummation that "ne'er shall fade nor fly." The Psalmist David had a similar vision:

> "There is none like thee among the gods, O Lord, nor are there any works like thine. All the nations thou hast made shall come and bow down before thee, O Lord, And shall glorify thy name. For thou art great and doest wondrous things, thou alone art God (Psa. 86:8 - 10)

His response is the only sensible one: "Teach me thy way, O Lord, that I may walk in thy truth; unite my heart to fear thy name." (Psa. 86:11) Similarly St. John, when in his vision he saw all things culminating in Christ and understood that the divine intentions for the universe are grand beyond the capacity of the human mind to receive, cried, "And I heard every creature in heaven and on earth and under the earth and in the sea, and all therein, saying 'To him who sits upon the throne and to the Lamb be blessing and honor and glory and might for ever and ever!' And the four living creatures said, 'Amen!' and the elders fell down and worshiped" (Rev. 5:13 - 14).

CHAPTER ELEVEN
THOSE TERRIBLE CHOICES

When I muse over the years I've spent in the garden, making flower beds, placing plants here and then there, I cannot help but be struck by the number of mistakes I have made. My life in the garden can almost be described as a series of attempts to correct poor choices, each year undoing or trying to do better what I perceive to have been wrong, or less then ideal, in last year's work. Had I a better imagination, perhaps many disappointments could have been avoided, but a weakness in my own personality is the need to see something in the actual world to know whether or not I like it. Many choices have been carefully and conscientiously made on drafting paper, only to be demonstrated as poor ones in reality.

Drive down any street in an established residential section and see the result of wrong choices in landscaping. Trees that were planted directly against a home now rise to roof level or tower above it, hiding windows and creating a general sense of neglect, sometimes of a macabre eeriness. Pillars of arborvitae are out of proportion and out of place. An abundance of bushes and shrubs create a sense of congestion and confusion because some landscaper was more interested in seeing how many plants he could sell rather than planting for the future. One can quickly make a long list of poor choices.

No doubt the original plantings were made for immediate effect and for the first year or two appeared satisfactory enough. It takes time for outcomes to manifest themselves. The day inevitably comes when the consequences of choices once made on the basis of expediency or haste or out of sheer ignorance appear, and changing them is difficult, sometimes even impossible. Precious time is always lost.

Happily, however, many mistakes can be corrected. The very nature of things offers a remedy. The cycle of the seasons, the steady march of the years, offer opportunities to try again, to do better. Unhappily, the number of recurring opportunities for any specific person is, after all, finite. Every gardener comes one day to the final season. But, until that occurs, one keeps trying, motivated by the challenge to make the next season better and the hope that this year's results are sure to be an improvement over the last.

Such, in microcosm, is the nature of life. Each day demands the making of any number of choices; in retrospect, some prove to have been right, others wrong. Right or wrong according to what standard? That's the crucial question. Only one standard is the true one, the will of God, the demands the Christian ideal holds out to us for right conduct. The Christian knows—or should know—what that is in abstract terms. "For this is the will of God, your sanctification: that you abstain from unchastity," Paul tells the Thessalonians (1 Thess.4:3). The Bible is full of precepts for living. The problem is to translate this knowledge into life, to make it fit the demands of our Mondays and Tuesdays and Wednesdays. We do our best, making choices in answer to this day's demands. In retrospect, some seem to have been right, some otherwise. And so we undertake to make the adjustments our judgment demands. Tomorrow will be better than today.

God knows and understands. He is easy to please, difficult to satisfy, as George MacDonald often observed. One may look upon one's life as at best a bungling affair and from a human perspective be unhappy with what it appears to be. Scripture reminds us that it is the set of the will, the intentions of the heart to keep trying, that count. It is God, not men, who takes the measure of success. Thank God for opportunities life affords to start over, to try to do things better, to make today an improvement upon yesterday. Thank Him also that the number of opportunities is finite, that there is a rest for the people of God, that in due season those will reap who have not fainted.

If, as Christianity most certainly teaches, we are destined to live somewhere forever, and if any given individual's future is shaped primarily by that person's choices, then our decisions are momentous affairs. Robert Browning, in his long poem "*The Ring and the Book*," has a Pope comment: "Life's business being just the terrible choice" (The Ring and the Book, 407). A startling statement, but so it is. By doing our best to choose wisely with consistency and by willing to be obedient we are promised to inherit great reward. "For to him who has will more be given, and he will have abundance; but from him who has not, even what he has will be taken away" (Matt. 13:12). George Herbert, whose talent includes applying a keen sense of the eternal to a close observation of everyday life and nature, has a fitting summary in his poem "Virtue":

> *Sweet day, so cool, so calm, so bright!*
> *The bridal of the earth and sky—*
> *The dew shall weep thy fall tonight;*
> *For thou must die.*
> *Sweet rose, whose hue angry and brave*
> *Bids the rash gazer wipe an eye,*
> *Thy root is ever in its grave,*
> *And thou must die.*
> *Sweet spring, full of sweet days and roses,*
> *A box where sweets compacted lie,*
> *My music shows ye have your closes,*

> *And all must die.*
> *Only a sweet and virtuous soul,*
> *Like season'd timber, never gives;*
> *But though the whole world turn to coal,*
> *Yet chiefly lives.*
> (Selected Poems of George Herbert, 65)

All a person sees, dies; virtue alone will live for time and eternity. Only those choices that issue in goodness really count.

CHAPTER TWELVE
THEREFORE I HAVE HOPE

Every summer it happens: temperatures of eighty-five degrees and higher, a few days of bright sun and drying wind, and the gardener eagerly consults each day's weather forecast, looks skyward, and longs for the respite of rain. Artificial watering may suffice for a time, but it is a nuisance to prepare for, in some areas costly, and, because water from the hose lacks the nitrogen of rain, using it is at best a stop-gap measure.

Hopes rise to a pitch of anticipation when a thunder shower is promised. But one can never be confident that the much-needed relief has come until sufficient water has actually fallen to satisfy the plants' requirements. Summer showers are often spasmodic and confined to areas of their own mysterious choosing. The emotional let down when showers are generally in the area but skirt one's premises is perhaps the most exasperating experience of gardening. Emily Dickinson describes such an occasion in "A Thunder-storm":

*The wind begun to rock the grass
With threatening tunes and low,--
He flung a menace at the earth,
A menace at the sky.*

*The leaves unhooked themselves from trees
And started all abroad;
The dust did scoop itself like hands
And threw away the road.*

*The wagons quickened on the streets,
The thunder hurried slow;
The lightning showed a yellow beak,
And then a livid claw.*

*The birds put up the bars to nests,
The cattle fled to barns;
There came one drop of giant rain,
And then, as if the hands*

*That held the dams had parted hold,
The waters wrecked the sky,
But overlooked my father's house,
Just quartering a tree.*

(Complete Poems of Emily Dickinson, 399)

The poet's refusal to describe her emotional letdown speaks more loudly than any attempt to detail it. What does she do? She wisely takes the larger view, exults in the stages of the event—after all, some people did benefit from the rain—and refrains from regret and self-pity.

To have such a reaction may not even occur to some. Nothing in life happens precisely according to one's expectations, and sometimes the contrary winds of adverse circumstances leave the soul as parched and despairing as withering plants. Wishing things otherwise is vain; self-pity is paralyzing. The Spirit of God would have one take the larger view, try to think of others rather than one's self, and look for the grace that is unfailingly present.

I remember as a child hearing an aunt frequently say, "There's never any great loss without some small gain." Often the gain to the soul is larger than one is aware. Personal disappointments, failures, and sufferings have the inevitable effect of prompting the soul to take a firmer hold upon God, realizing that, after all, only that which has to do with our life in Him really matters. George MacDonald remarked: "So sure am I that many things which illness has led me to see are true, that I would endlessly rather never be well than lose sight of them" (Paul Faber, 256).

Who can speak with more authority on this subject than Jeremiah who, in the midst of all the agonies and afflictions of his ministry, affirmed: "Remember my affliction and my bitterness, the wormwood and the gall! My soul continually thinks of it and is bowed down within me. But this I call to mind, and therefore I have hope: The steadfast love of the Lord never ceases, his mercies never come to an end; they are new every morning; great is thy faithfulness. 'The Lord is my portion,' says my soul, 'therefore I will hope in him'" (Lam. 3:19 - 24).

CHAPTER THIRTEEN
SHOWERS OF BLESSING

How glorious rain is! Television weather forecasters have it all wrong when they compose a long face and predict an ordeal of showers. Any gardener rejoices in rain and would much prefer a wet year to a dry one. What sound is so pleasant as to awake at night and hear the sound of a gentle rain upon the leaves outside the bedroom window? All nature rejoices in it. Or to hear, on a day in July, the faint sound of thunder in the distance, see the darker clouds slowly mounting from the West, and then begin receiving first, the sprinkles, then the steadily increasing rain, to be followed by the returning sunshine and the life-celebrating smell of the refreshed earth. Emily Dickinson gives memorable expression to the exhilarating experience in "Summer Shower":

A drop fell on the apple tree,
Another on the roof;
A half a dozen kissed the eaves,
And made the gables laugh.

A few went out to help the brook,
That went to help the sea.
Myself conjectured, Were they pearls,
What necklaces could be!

The dust replaced in hoisted roads,
The birds jocoser sung;
The sunshine threw his hat away,
The orchards spangles hung.

The breezes brought dejected lutes
And bathed them in the glee;
The East put out a single flag,
And signed the fete away.
(Complete Poems of Emily Dickinson, 387)

A summer shower renewing the earth is an apt metaphor for the refreshment of the spirit that comes periodically to every faithful believer. An old hymn begins, "There shall be showers of blessing, Blessed reviving again, Over the hills and the valleys, Sound of abundance of rain." The imagery comes from a long passage, Ezekiel 34, that presents God as the Shepherd that will supply all the needs of His sheep: "And I will make them and the places round about my hill a blessing; and I will send down the showers in their season; they shall be showers of blessing. And

the trees of the field shall yield their fruit, and the
earth shall yield its increase, and they shall be secure
in their land; and they shall know that I am the
Lord..." (vv. 26, 27). Although the passage applies
most directly to the future state of the Kingdom, it
speaks most graphically to the gardener who knows
the beauty of summer showers.

The normal Christian life inevitably has periods
of doubt and perplexity, but these are more then
balanced by those moments of joy and peace that are
accompanied with deep convictions of the realities of
faith. The former periods are multiplied when the mind
is fixed upon the self and self-concerns, the latter
when the attention is directed toward praise for God's
blessings and concern for the needs of others. Every
moment has its duty as regards our relationship to
someone; to address these obligations willingly with
the help of God is to receive the gift of joy His pleasure
alone can bestow. "From of old no one has heard or
perceived by the ear, no eye has seen a God besides
thee, who works for those who wait for him. Thou
meetest him that joyfully works righteousness, those
that remember thee in thy ways" (Isa. 64:4, 5).

One's outward state or condition need have nothing to do with the periods of inner refreshment the Spirit of God sends. Dostoevsky's Dimitri Karamazov in prison awaiting trial for a crime he did not commit exults to his visiting brother concerning his hope as a Christian, ". . . in our great sorrow, we shall rise again to joy, without which man cannot live nor God exist, for God gives joy: it's His privilege—a grand one. Ah, man should be dissolved in prayer! What should I be . . . without God?" (*The Brothers Karamazov*, 720). True joy, so different from happiness as such, is a gift God alone gives, a gift sometimes bestowed amid outward circumstances seemingly so incongruous with inner well-being.

CHAPTER FOURTEEN
REALITY

The pleasure I receive from my garden comes mainly from simply contemplating it, letting the beauty of a blossom have its full effect upon my spirit. To behold the beauty and receive the fragrance of a bearded iris is to know a host of pleasant feelings. A person can bring into a garden all sorts of mental rubbish—stresses, resentments, untoward thoughts—and have it all purged by fixing one's attention upon a simple bloom. The demons one has brought can be replaced with a spirit of awe, delight, and hope.

The poet William Wordsworth affirms how, when the imagination is actively perceiving the reality at the heart of the created world, the conviction arises that

> *Our destiny, our being's heart and home,*
> *Is with infinitude, and only there;*
> *With hope it is, hope that can never die;*
> *Effort, and expectation, and desire,*
> *And something evermore about to be.*
> (William Wordsworth, 464)

Moments spent contemplating a garden can have such effect. They quicken the feeling that we were not made for death but have an eternal destiny, and they strengthen that sublime expectation that a greater good is yet to come. They cleanse and invigorate the spirit.

Where but in a garden can one find more pure expressions of natural beauty, and where can the mystery of things be felt more keenly? What is seen shows something unseen. The writer of the book of Hebrews affirms, "By faith we understand that the world was created by the word of God, so that what is seen was made out of things which do not appear (11:3)." To see a garden rightly is to perceive something of the Word of God by which it was made. You too will see it, if you look. That is a glimpse of Reality. The only true reality is spiritual reality, reality with a capital "R."

Perhaps the most alarming aspect of modern life is its determined attempts to take our attention away from Reality. This is obvious in the way the silliness of contemporary advertising appeals solely to base desires, assuring us that their fulfillment lies in acquiring more material things or having the most satisfying sexual experience. That's all life is about. The hectic pace of modern life consumes our time, economic concerns drive our decisions. We fill our lives with stuff, more stuff, bigger and newer stuff, and brazenly move from one partner to another. But all that will pass, and the soul that has fed only upon husks will in the end find itself impoverished indeed. "The world passes away, and the lust of it; but he who does the will of God abides for ever" (1 John. 2:17).

Reality can also, and in a more subtle and insidious way, be obscured by mere rational knowledge about things. Information about a thing, as soon as it is substituted for an appreciation of the thing itself, somehow gets in the way and removes one from what is. Knowing the full botanical name of a flower and correctly identifying all the parts of its bloom can, if one is not careful, detract from an imaginative reception of its beauty.

W. B. Yeats, in contemplating the stony stares of statues in an art gallery, mused, "Empty eyeballs knew / That knowledge increases unreality. . . ."(*Collected Poems of W.B. Yeats*, 323) After having exercised in his poetry throughout his life his remarkable imaginative talent and intellectual capacity, Yeats concluded: "Neither loose imagination, / Nor the mill of the mind / Consuming its rag and bone, / Can make the truth known"(*Ibid.*, 299). Both his intellect and his imagination had failed him. The person who knows the Creator God and sees the world as a direct product of His hand does not share such despair. His knowledge extends quite beyond rational analysis to an intuitive apprehension of what truly is. My garden has provided me with a powerful antidote for skepticism and nihilistic attitudes.

A true appreciation for natural reality can, in a mysterious and unfathomable way, lead ones' attention to eternal Reality, at the heart of which is Christ. In her poem "Reality," Frances Ridley Havergal accurately expresses that central truth:

> *Reality, reality,*
> *Lord Jesus Christ Thou art to me!*
> *From the spectral mist and the driving clouds,*
> *From the shifting shadows and phantom crowds*
> *From unreal words and unreal lives,*
> *Where truth with falsehood feebly strives;*
> *From the passings away, the chance and change,*
> *Flickerings, vanishings, swift and strange,*
>
>> *I turn to my glorious rest in Thee,*
>> *Who art the grand Reality!...*
>
> *Reality, reality,*
> *Lord Jesus Christ is crowned in Thee,*
> *In Thee is every type fulfilled*
> *In Thee is every yearning stilled*

> *For perfect beauty, truth and love:*
> *For Thou art always far above*
> *The grandest glimpse of our Ideal,*
> *Yet more and more we know Thee real,*
> > *And marvel more and more to see*
> > *Thine infinite Reality...*
> ("Hill," *The World's Great Religious Poetry*, 325)

Dirt is real. The mystery of growth, the beauty of fruit and flower, the satisfactions of honest labor—these are real. They are real because they were created and are sustained by Christ, "for in him all things were created, in heaven and on earth, visible and invisible, whether thrones or dominions or principalities or authorities-all things were created through him and for him. He is before all things, and in him all things hold together" (Col. 1:16, 17). In Him the real and the Real coalesce.

CHAPTER FIFTEEN
THE MOMENTS SATAN CANNOT FIND

Of all the times to be in the garden, the early morning is the best. At dawn the golden light of the rising sun touches first the tops of the trees, then gradually, silently slips down, branch by branch, to the boles, to the ground. It floods the landscape with a freshness and sparkle that renew and invigorate the spirit. All is serene, all is quiet, save for the awakening birds whose morning songs speak so purely of peace and joy.

William Blake was in his garden at Felpham in the early morning, rejoicing in the rising sun, when he affirmed:

> *There is a moment in each day*
> *that Satan cannot find*
> *Nor can his watch fiends find it,*
> *but the industrious find*
> *This moment and it multiply,*
>
> *and when it once is found*
> *It renovates every moment of the day*
> *if rightly placed.*
> (*Complete Poetry and Prose of* William Blake, 136)

It is in the early morning when one is most likely to have such moments "that Satan cannot find," and they can indeed affect the way one faces the entire day. Opening one's spirit to Christ at the outset of each day is indispensable to knowing the grace and peace that God wants to give and will give if we but allow Him the opportunity. Meeting God in one's garden in the cool of the morning seems to bring a yet fuller outpouring of strength sufficient for that day's need. The quiet beauty of the dawning day powerfully suggests the promise of the ever-growing good that awaits the obedient child of God: "The path of the just is as the shining light, that shineth more and more unto the perfect day." (Prov. 4:18, *King James Version*)

Those moments of deepened thought and insight, moments of spiritual illumination sometimes called epiphanies, come most readily in times of solitude in which the spirit turns from mundane concerns to simple gratitude for life and consciousness and well-being. John

Masefield referred to them as "moments of the soul in years of earth" and built his long poem "Biography" around them, recalling those "golden instants" from his own past when "life became more splendid than its husk," and his soul was enlarged. He wrote:

> *Men do not heed the rungs by which men climb*
> *Those glittering steps, those milestones upon Time,*
> *Those tombstones of dead selves, those hours of birth,*
> *Those moments of the soul in years of earth. . .*
> (Poems, 192)

Surely it is difficult to talk of them, even to a close friend, but everyone who listens to life knows these golden minutes do indeed occur. In his long poem The Four Quartets T. S. Eliot organized his meditations around such illumined moments. The first occurred for him imaginatively in a rose garden, in which he sensed the presence of the spirits of the redeemed, the Triumphant Dead:

> *Footfalls echo in the memory*
> *Down the passage which we did not take*
> *Towards the door we never opened*
> *Into the rose-garden. My words echo*
> *Thus in your mind. . . .*
>
> *Other echoes*
> *Inhabit the garden. Shall we follow? . . . .*
> *There they were, dignified, invisible,*
> *Moving without pressure, over the dead leaves,*

> *In the autumn heat, through the vibrant air . . .*
> (*Complete Poems and Plays*, "Burnt Norton," 117)

Eliot's imagination was haunted by the dignified presence of redeemed spirits that were more real by the very fact they were invisible. We are the poorer when we are oblivious to the truth that, as the writer of the letter to the Hebrews tells us, "we are surrounded by so great a cloud of witnesses" (Heb. 12:1), the spirits of just people now made perfect (12:23).

When in the final quartet Eliot came to the chapel of Little Gidding to worship, he again felt their presence and heard a voice speak to his spirit:

> *You are here to kneel*
> *Where prayer has been valid. And prayer is more*
> *Than an order of words, the conscious occupation*
> *Of the praying mind, or the sound of the voice praying.*
> *And what the dead had no speech for, when living,*
> *They can tell you, being dead: the communication*
> *Of the dead is tongued with fire beyond the language*
> *of the living.*
> ("Little Gidding," *Ibid.*, 139)

Such experiences are often referred to as mystic and are thought to be reserved for the devout. But they are available to all who earnestly respond to the invitation, "Let us then with confidence draw near to the throne of grace, that we may receive mercy and find grace to help in time of need" (Heb. 4:16). To wait in trust and expectation before God is not to be disappointed.

CHAPTER SIXTEEN
WAITING FOR THE HARVEST

As autumn approaches, the rewards of all one's efforts are on every hand. This is what it's all about. To be sure, some hopes have not been realized—the basil never germinated (was it planted too early?), and the watermelons tasted poor (was the variety right for that particular soil?). Failures, however, are more than compensated for by the wealth of successes.

Flowers are outdoing themselves with masses of color: breathtakingly red canna heads tower over crowds of marigolds and mums, while gigantic dahlias in all pastel shades proudly nod in the afternoon sun. Lusciously red tomatoes hang expectantly on sprawling vines; squash and cucumbers, beets and carrots, all seem vying to be the first prepared for the dinner table. It all reminds one of the abundance of the grace of God, the sheer superabundance of His bounty. He has met the labor of planning, planting, weeding and mulching with more than ample reward. (I however, resolve, not to plant quite so many vegetables next year—too much goes to waste.)

The metaphors of reaping and harvesting abound in Scripture. Christ speaks of the importance of winning people to Himself in such terms: "I tell you, lift up your eyes, and see how the fields are already white for harvest. He who reaps receives wages, and gathers fruit for eternal life... (John 4:35, 36). In urging the need to be liberal in giving, Paul writes: "He who sows sparingly will also reap sparingly, and he who sows bountifully will also reap bountifully.... He who supplies seed to the sower and bread for food will supply and multiply your resources and increase the harvest of your righteousness" (2 Cor. 9:6, 10). And in encouraging the Galatians to be consistent and patient, he writes: "Do not be deceived; God is not mocked, for whatever a man sows, that he will also reap.... And let us not grow weary in well-doing, for in due season we shall reap, if we do not lose heart" (Gal. 6:7, 9).

Everything one does in the garden either issues in harvest or wasted effort, and so it is with life. The Bible offers the promise of ample reward for those who overcome, both to encourage the patient practice of righteous living and also to assure us of the ample compensation for all the pain and agonies we endure. "I consider that the sufferings of this present time are not worth comparing with the glory that is to be revealed to us," Paul concludes (Rom. 8: 18). Robert Browning summarizes: "By the pain-throb, triumphantly winning intensified bliss, / And the next world's reward and repose, by the struggles in this" (*Pippa Passes and Shorter Poems*, 404).

One reason why gardening metaphors abound in the Bible is that life on this earth is but the preliminary phase, the preparation and beginning of the harvest that is to come. The activities and pursuits for the advancement of the Kingdom that consume much of the faithful Christian's time and effort are like seeding and cultivating and fertilizing plants. It's all done for the future harvest of which the Christian has a vision of delight—delight because the Great Gardener of Souls will be delighted, and the faithful worker will share in that delight.

Much of the wonder of harvesting fruit comes from the realization that somehow all fruits and flowers in their infinite variety emerge from the mystery of creation and growth. Dulcet, deeply red strawberries nestled in the strawy mulch; sweet luscious plums on heavily laden branches; meaty, plump tomatoes hanging in great clusters on proud and stately plants: from where have they come? We take the miracle of their appearance as a matter of course, seldom giving any thought to how they could possibly come into being. Soil and water, air and gardener's toil have mysteriously combined to produce them, but none of these elements contains the slightest hint or indication that, by acting upon a minute seed planted just a few months ago, these marvels would appear. No novice imagination, seeing the process for the first time, could in its wildest reaches have foreseen such results.

What explanation is more satisfying to the Christian mind than that all that is harvested is an expression of the loveliness of God latent in his creation, a loveliness unimaginable and imperceptible until it is beheld and tasted, a loveliness abundantly adequate to gratify hunger and delight existence itself? In its startling unpredictability and its capacity to give endless delight and satisfaction, it is a striking metaphor of heaven. Paul, in speaking of the "secret and hidden wisdom of God" writes: "But, as it is written, 'What no eye has seen, nor ear heard, nor the heart of man conceived, what God has prepared for those who

love him,' God has revealed to us through the Spirit."
(1 Cor. 2:9, 10) The harvest will be an astounding
and delightful manifestation of God's power and
graciousness. One of the passages Paul is referring
to presents God as saying "For behold, I create new
heavens and a new earth; and the former things shall
not be remembered or come into mind. But be glad
and rejoice for ever in that which I create, for behold, I
create Jerusalem a rejoicing, and her people a joy. (Isa.
65:17, 18) In pondering Paul's affirmation that believers
shall share in "the inheritance of the saints in light"
(Col. 1:12), George MacDonald wrote:

> Heaven will be continuous touch with God. The
> very sense of being will in itself be bliss. For the
> sense of true life, there must be actual, conscious
> contact with the source of the life; therefore mere
> life—in itself, in its very essence good—good as the
> life of God which is our life—must be such bliss as, I
> think, will need the mitigation of the loftiest joys of
> communion with our blessed fellows; the mitigation
> of art in every shape.... The bliss of pure being
> will, I say, need these mitigations to render the
> intensity of it endurable by heart and brain. ("The
> Inheritance," *Unspoken Sermons: Third Series*, 610, 616)

It was in the anticipation of such bliss that Christ
endured the cross. "The joy that was set before him"
(Heb. 12:2) will be realized in full measure at the
consummation of all things, the harvest of the ages,

a joy in which all believers will participate. Therefore, the trials, injustices, and inequalities we experience here and now that occasion so much suffering and bewilderment; the mistakes even the best people make that precipitate so much guilt and regret; the sudden deaths and seemingly tragic events that completely deplete the spirit—all these can be absorbed in the consciousness that, because we are partakers with Christ in the life eternal, we will see in the ages to come how all events will have contributed to the reaping. The harvest will be abundant.

Abundant, that is, for all whose faith and sacrifices in this life have readied them to receive such further expression of the grace of God. Just as no gardener expects great results without having exerted the necessary effort and skill, so eternal rewards are dependent upon present faithfulness. A facile presentation of Christianity may suggest that the rewards for right living may be expected here and now, but such is not the Biblical vision. Suffering here is inevitable. But because of the wedding of justice with mercy that God will effect in the ages to come, there will finally be no disappointments, only affirmation and joy. Scripture counsels us to be patient for that which will come in due time. The abundant life enables the Christian to face all that life offers—not without emotional turmoil, certainly, but with an ability to work through such events to peace, a stronger faith, and a quiet expectation for the harvest God has promised. For he has "raised us up with him, and made us sit with him in the heavenly places in Christ Jesus, that in the coming ages he might show the immeasurable riches of his grace in kindness toward us in Christ Jesus" (Eph. 2:6, 7).

CHAPTER SEVENTEEN
OUT OF EVIL, GOOD

It's an autumn day, cool and overcast, but the air is invigorating. Frost has killed the annuals and blackened the perennials. Even the late-blooming mums and asters are over. It's time to make fresh compost, that "black gold" that is indispensable to successful gardening.

Some sort of bin or container is necessary. A person can purchase steel bins, if one is so inclined, which are generally suspended above ground on an iron frame with a handle for periodic turning. Advertisements boast that they make compost in fourteen days. Perhaps. It all depends upon what materials are used and how often one turns the bin. I'm highly skeptical, and I don't care to spend that kind of money on the project. Such expense is not necessary. A very suitable bin can be made of reasonably heavy fencing and four corner stakes, and, as for the fourteen days, I think it wiser to plan to use the compost made this season next spring.

I prefer wooden bins. They look neater, are not too expensive to build, and will last for several years. I've made mine out of strips of cedar lumber, one-inch by two-inch by four-feet, screwed (not nailed) to four two-inch by two-inch corner stakes. The strips are fastened to the corner posts at two inch intervals. This ensures that the compost has a maximum amount of air. Air is just as essential to the composting process as it is to any fire. The front panel is made to match, the one-inch by two-inch by four-foot cedar strips screwed to two upright ones, designed to slide up and down between wood slat tracks. My bins are four feet high.

At least two bins should be placed side by side if the intention is to turn the materials. Turning is simply the process of forking them from one bin to another for the purpose of allowing air to activate the decomposition. The more times one does this at intervals of a couple weeks or so, the quicker the decomposing takes place. A five-tine—or what we referred to on the farm as a manure fork—is the necessary tool for the task.

If turning proves a too forbidding chore, compost can still be made without it. The decomposition simply takes longer—somewhat over a year, depending upon the materials used. If one makes three compost bins, one each fall, and does no turning, the first is ready for use by the third spring. Thereafter a person has a bin of compost to use each year.

My wife Dorothy and I keep an enclosed plastic

pail just outside the kitchen door for depositing all fruit and vegetable waste, together with tea and coffee grounds. As soon as the pail is full it is emptied into the compost bin. All summer we put all garden waste in the same bin, careful not to include any weeds that have gone to seed. In the autumn I add to the pile all the frost- blackened plants from the garden beds, together with the shredded leaves that I bagged throughout October with the lawnmower. Horse manure, if available, makes a great additive, the bedding being a fine soil conditioner.

I "make" the compost by adding these plant materials to the bin in layers of about six inches each, covering each layer with a bag of stable waste, which amounts to about two inches. An alternative is to add a layer of soil, with perhaps a sprinkling (not too much!) of general purpose commercial fertilizer to activate decomposition and enrich the mixture. The water hose is handy to wet each layer. I'm careful not to add too much fertilizer so as to avoid making the mixture too "hot" or high in nutrients, with the result that plants to which the compost is later applied will grow all leaves and no flowers or fruits. If the bin is full of the new mixture before all the collected ingredients are used, I wait two or three weeks until the bin settles, then finish the job.

In the early spring—or in the late fall if the weather and my inclinations are right—I will turn the material by forking it into an empty bin. Later in the spring the compost is well made and ready to be applied to the garden beds. It is deep black, crumbly, almost fluffy, with a wonderful humusy smell. A little goes a long way. One readily sees the difference during the growing season in stronger, happier plants with more flowers or fruit. When the bin is empty, it is ready to receive a new batch of materials; and the process of recycling continues.

People who burn or otherwise dispose of leaves and garden waste do themselves and their beds or lawns a great disservice. Compost not only brings nutrients to the soil but also acts as a necessary mediator, giving the soil tilth, which enables plants to absorb the nutrients they need. No amount of commercial fertilizer will condition the soil so well, giving it the loose fluffy texture that compost will. Soil that lacks the necessary tilth can have nutrients in it that plants cannot properly access, the essential bacteria in compost being absent. Well-composted soil also has better drainage, enabling it to retain the proper amount of water for plant growth and at the same time preventing it from becoming water-logged, which gives the plants wet feet, poor root growth, and the inevitable rot that kills them.

The mystery of the composting procedure is not unlike the mystery that is ever taking place in the spiritual world; that is, out of the moral debris of life good is constantly emerging. The difficulties, the reverses, the challenges of life inspire the effort that overcomes and secures the prize. Tragedies can effect changes of heart. Pride can give way to humility, envy to pity, cold indifference to kindly concern. God is in the shadows, governing the process, and He calls upon His children to help Him in the great enterprise. With the proper discernment, we can be co-laborers with him, encouraging the righteousness He loves.

When Milton's Satan, freshly cast upon the floor of hell and determined to accomplish his revenge upon God, instructed his followers, he commissioned them:

> . . . *If then his Providence*
> *Out of evil seek to bring forth good,*
> *Our labor must be to pervert that end,*
> *And out of good still to find means of evil.*
> (*Complete Poems and Major Prose*, 215)

Milton's words succinctly express the essence of the spiritual warfare that is constantly raging. No disappointment or defeat, no catastrophe or disaster occurs but what some good ensues from its rubble. As in the garden, the volume of debris may appear much greater than the good that seemingly accrues, but it is God, not us, who measures the true value of any given good. The main point is the mysterious process can be greatly augmented by those who see and seize the opportunities. To be Christian is to have eyes to discern the spiritual struggle, to realize the momentousness of it, and to lend one's energies to help produce the good.

To ask why God allows such workings to continue, in light of the horrific effects of evil, is to glimpse something of the premium God places upon the righteousness the strategy produces.

> *. . . famished field and blackened tree*
> *Bear flowers in Eden never known*
> *Blossoms of grief and charity*
> *Bloom in these darkened fields alone.*
> *What had Eden ever to say*
> *Of hope and faith and pity and love*
> *Until was buried all its day*
> *And memory found its treasure trove?*
> *Strange blessings never in Paradise*
> *Fall from these beclouded skies.*
> (Collected Poems: 1921-1951, 190)

Faith and hope, pity and love are precious realities that can be fully realized only in a fallen world. To count the cost and object to the expense is to challenge the wisdom of Calvary.

CHAPTER EIGHTEEN
WHAT I DO IS ME

"However do you do all the work?" is perhaps the question most often asked by visitors to my gardens. The remark always takes me back a bit, as I really do not see the time spent in gardening as in any way burdensome or onerous. I want to do it, find more enjoyment in doing it than in anything else, and so I do it. Physically exhausting it most certainly is, and the older I get the more quickly I feel the exhaustion. But there is something delicious about being thoroughly tired. The cushions on the chaise lounge on the patio, or the gentle swaying of a hammock in the shade of a tree, are never properly appreciated until one is physically ready for them.

Work is good for the soul as well as the body. Paul speaks sternly concerning those who shirk their duties and try to avoid work. Anyone who does not work should not be allowed to eat. The decree that God made to Adam and Eve after the Fall, that they must henceforth "toil" and eat bread "in the sweat of your face" is often viewed as a curse, and no doubt it was in the relative sense of comparing their new lives with those they knew in their prelapsarian state. But even so, God had placed them in Eden "to till and keep it," which certainly required attention and effort. God's decree after their disobedience, like all His actions, was motivated by love for His creatures and prompted by His divine sense of what would be indispensable to whole and completed lives. In his poem "Hoeing," John Updike muses on the value of that simple task:

> *I sometimes fear the younger*
> *generation will be deprived*
> *of the pleasures of hoeing;*
> *there is no knowing*
> *how many souls have been formed*
> *by this simple exercise.*
>
> *The dry earth like a great scab breaks, revealing*
> *moist-dark loam—*
> *the pea-roots home,*
> *a fertile wound perpetually healing.*
>
> *How neatly the green weeds go under!*
> *The blade chops the earth new.*
> *Ignorant the wise boy who*
> *has never performed this simple, stupid, and useful*
> *wonder.*
> (Collected Poems: 1953-1993, 91)

Work is necessary for us to become whole persons, completing what we are. It is unfortunate that so many people do not enjoy the work they do. The downside of our industrial/technological society is that many jobs are repetitive and boring. Nevertheless, one large difference, it seems to me, between those who enjoy what they do and those who do not is often (not always) one of attitude. God stands ready to help all of us here. All jobs are, in some aspect at least, a means of service, of contributing positively to the lives of others. They can be, in other words, expressions of love, and learning to love is what life is all about. When in his poem "The Little Black Boy," William Blake wrote: "And we are put on earth a little space,/That we may learn to bear the beams of love. . ."(*Complete Poetry and Prose of William Blake*, 10) he succinctly captured the essence and purpose of life.

The meaning of our lives is shaped by our learning how to love in our everyday affairs. The two basic commandments, which encompass all others, are to love God and to love people. To see whatever job one has as a means of learning how to love and with one's efforts to express it is the first step toward finding the fulfillment for life's purpose and goal.

Hamlet's remark that "there is nothing either good or bad but thinking makes it so" (*The Yale Shakespeare*, 63) has dubious application in any metaphysical sense, but in terms of the importance of attitude it rings true. It is not only foolish but seriously self-defeating not to attempt to think positively toward whatever one's lot in life is. God, who by His Spirit stands ready to work "for good with those who love him" (Rom. 8:28), is stymied when we persist in fixing our minds upon the underside of things. Paul's final entreaty to the Christians at Philippi, "whatever is true, whatever is honorable, whatever is just, whatever is pure, whatever is lovely, whatever is gracious, if there is any excellence, if there is anything worthy of praise, think about these things"(Phil. 4:8) is a sure remedy for the doldrums of self-pity.

Not only so, but a person's work defines what that person is, and our individuality is such that each person can do something in life better than can anyone else. God calls us to develop that side of our personality. In one of his fine sonnets, Gerard Manley Hopkins notes the distinct singularity of everything in God's creation and applies it to the Christian's calling:

> *As kingfishers catch fire, dragonflies draw flame;*
> *As tumbled over rim in roundy wells*
> *Stones ring; like each tucked string tells, each hung*
> *Bow swung finds tongue to fling out broad its name;*
> *Each mortal thing does one thing and the same;*
> *Deals out that being indoors each one dwells;*
> *Selves-goes itself; myself it speaks and spells,*
> *Crying What I do is me: for that I came.*

> *I say more: the just man justices;*
> > *Keeps grace: that keeps all his goings graces;*
> *Acts in God's eye what in God's eye he is—*
> > *Christ. For Christ plays in ten thousand places,*
> *Lovely in limbs, and lovely in eyes not his*
> > *To the Father through the features of men's faces.*
> (Poems of Gerald Manley Hopkins, 90)

"What I do is me: for that I came" succinctly expresses a startling truth. To see one's being as standing at a great distance from what one does day after day is a serious exercise in self-deception. When one stands at the Judgment, as all most certainly will, there will be no distance between what one is and what one has done.

Whatever job one has, the daily opportunities it presents to do good are invitations from God to work with Him for someone's benefit. They may be as seemingly insignificant as a smile to a fellow worker or a gracious word when a sharp one could have been given, but in the grace of God who knows what momentous eternal effect it may have. Acts that are ostensibly trivial in our estimation, like the cup of cold water, are large in his. Edwin Muir wrote:

> *For small is great and great is small,*
> *And a blind seed all.*
> ("The Road," Collected Poems, 42)

So God works. Paul counseled:

> "But God chose what is foolish in the world to shame the wise, God chose what is weak in the world to shame the strong, God chose what is low and despised in the world, even things that are not, to bring to nothing things that are, so that no human being might boast in the presence of God" (1 Cor. 1: 27 - 28).

Believing this is a vital part of faith and indispensable to effective Christian service.

CHAPTER NINETEEN
WINTER DOLDRUMS

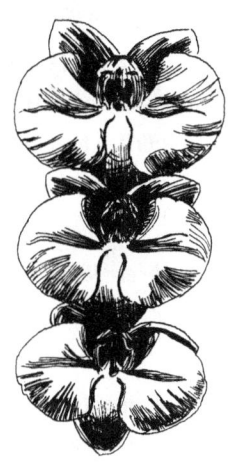

For most gardeners, I think, winter is a season to be endured with patience at best, boredom at worst. It opposes growth; and, although a person may be convinced it has beauties unique to it, such as figurations of snow, the ground beneath is barren and desolate. For poets and artists, winter is a ready image for depletion and sterility, together with its accompanying moods of desolation and loneliness.

It was so for Robert Frost in his poem "Desert Places":

> Snow falling and night falling fast, oh, fast
> In a field I looked into going past,
> And the ground almost covered smooth in snow,
> But a few weeds and stubble showing last.
>
> The woods around it have it—it is theirs.
> All animals are smothered in their lairs.
> I am too absent-spirited to count;
> The loneliness includes me unawares.
>
> And lonely as it is, that loneliness
> Will be more lonely ere it will be less—
> A blanker whiteness of benighted snow
> With no expression, nothing to express.
>
> They cannot scare me with their empty spaces
> Between stares-on stares where no human race is.
> I have it in me so much nearer home
> To scare myself with my own desert places.
> (Complete Poems, Prose & Plays, 269)

Loneliness is itself a terrible state, a foretaste, I think, of the desolations of outer darkness that our Lord warned awaits those who will not have God in their knowledge. An eternal winter, with no hope of spring. Praise God for the escape available in His grace.

The Christian life, nevertheless, can have its doldrums. We are creatures of emotions, and emotions have their ups and downs. Often our "downs" may puzzle us, as they can occur in the midst of apparent well-being when one can discern no outward cause for them. They may even generate guilt: "I am a Christian. What is the matter with me, that I am depressed?" The Psalmist knew such an experience when he questioned: "Why are you cast down, O my soul, and why are you disquieted within me?" (Psa. 42: 5)

Moments of euphoria can be just as arbitrary. One can even know moments of joy and lightness of heart during times of reversal and hardship. We cannot control our emotions, and they cannot always be accounted for. Unless a person's state is extreme (in which case help should be sought), one can will to act in the face of moods and not be at their mercy.

So often, at the heart of a person's doldrums is a fixation on the self that generates the emotional detritus of self-pity. Physical inertia and emotional paralysis set in. The remedy is at hand: do something. There is something other than serving the self that God would have you do—now. Address the duty of the moment, asking God to help.

George MacDonald, a man who increasingly experienced periods of euphoria followed by depression as he aged, wrote:

> *Therefore, O Lord, when all things common seem,*
> *When all is dust, and self the center clod,*

> *When grandeur is a hopeless, foolish dread,*
> *And anxious care more reasonable than God.--*
> *Out of Job's ashes I will call to thee-*
> *In spite of dread distrust call earnestly-*
> *O thou who livest, call, then answer dying me.*
> (The Diary of an Old Soul, August 31, 113)

His prayer echoes the depressed Psalmist's advice to himself: "Hope in God; for I shall again praise him, my help and my God. My soul is cast down within me, therefore I remember thee..." (Psa. 42:5, 6) MacDonald observes elsewhere that when people think they are tired of life, it is death, not life, they are tired of.

When spiritual doldrums set in, pray, and then do something that takes the mind off of the self. Shop for some gloxinias, or buy and prepare another amaryllis bulb. The life of plants, the urge of things to grow, are reminders of the natural life that courses through the universe. They are as well analogues of that higher life that God bestows upon those who are faithful in doing his will. And working with them is a means of grace.

Just as escape from eternal desolation may be found in the grace of God, escape from temporal boredom can be had in the home. People who love plants must grow them all through the year. The winter months present a challenge easily met. Many plants, readily available in garden centers and general merchandise stores, will quickly reward correct horticultural practices and a little patient care. An amaryllis, for example, is easily grown and is unsurpassed for beauty in the home. African violets, clivia lilies, phalaenopsis (moth orchids), and gloxinias are but a few examples of happy choices that will reward proper care with weeks of indoor beauty.

Instructions for successfully growing such plants are near at hand, available with the purchases, whether one buys them locally or through mail order sources. Because such rules are necessarily generalized and often "run of the mill," the purchaser can expect some failures and must learn from them. If what you did last year did not work, don't give up; carefully think through what might have gone wrong and try again. My own experience has taught me several things:

PURCHASING. Buy good stock. Discount houses may be an acceptable source, but be wary. Workers too often neglect to care properly for plants on their counters, and the risk for failure in purchasing stunted plants is large. Low prices are always tempting, but one is gambling with one's time, effort, and money. If a person is fortunate enough to be present when plants newly arrive, the risk is much less. Plants purchased directly from a greenhouse are worth the extra money.

Most mail order sources are reliable, but not all. Immediately send back any plant material that is questionable or inferior with a note asking for replacement or a full refund, including postage. If they want to keep you as a customer, they will try to please. Even so, purchases are best made at established nurseries and garden centers where you can see what you are getting.

TEMPERATURE. Do be careful here. Many plants react violently when exposed to extreme cold or heat. Protect them adequately in transport and situate them properly in the home. Protect them from drafts. Most house plants like daytime temperatures in the seventies and nighttime in the low sixties. Cool is better than hot, especially at night. Window sills generally work well; add a shelf if needed.

POTTING. Newly purchased plants should be checked to see if they need repotting. Gently remove them from their container; tap the side of the pot, turn it upside down, and, suspending the plant between your fingers, gently remove the pot. If the roots are abundant and look congested, so that they have begun to grow in circles, repot. Congested roots should be cut off or, if your new pot is large enough, spread out so that they do not continue to grow in a circle.

Proper potting soil may be purchased, or, if you prefer to mix your own, use equal parts pulverized garden soil, spaghum peat moss, and perlite. Add a balanced, time-release fertilizer according to directions. Select a pot one inch larger than the prior one. Too large a container will not provide the plant proper drainage, and the plant will not do well. Be certain the new pot has ample drain holes; cover them with a few pieces of shard, that is, broken pottery. Gently pack the soil around the plant to remove the air pockets and place it out of direct sunlight for a couple days before moving it to its permanent location. Plants vary as to their need for and tolerance of winter sun, but all need ample light. A location well-lit with indirect lighting—not more than a couple hours of direct sun daily—will work well for most house plants.

WATERING. Nothing kills a potted plant more quickly than over-watering. The rule of thumb is, do not water a pot until the surface is dry. It should then be amply watered. Check your plants each day; the first sign of wilting of the leaves is a distress signal. Some plants need to be kept moist, others respond well to periodic dry periods. My clivia lilies get two six week periods with no water each year, one during December and January, the other during July and August. They reward me with blooms almost immediately upon my resuming ample watering. My potted agapanthus plants, which I take inside before frost each fall, are kept utterly dry until they are returned to my patio the following spring. Then, watered profusely, they respond with a plethora of stately blue umbels.

Use water that is of room temperature but has not been sitting inside for days, and avoid softened water. Water collected from outside, such as melted snow or rainwater, is best, as it naturally contains minerals plants love. Be certain the soil you are wetting drains quickly. Never use a pot that does not have generous drain holes in the bottom, and use shard in the bottom of all pots. Set the pots in drain pans but don't let them sit in water.

Plants will respond to extra humidity, and for some, such as ferns, it is a must. Situate the pot on a tray filled with pea gravel and keep the gravel moist. Or purchase a room humidifier and keep it near the plants.

FERTILIZING. Keep your plants growing with light applications of a balanced fertilizer. The three numbers on the container identify, in order, nitrogen, phosphate and potash. For general use they should be approximately the same, such as 12-12-12. For spring growth, the first number should be the highest; for later in the season, to encourage bloom, the second and third numbers should be highest. Be careful to follow directions, erring--if any--on the low side. Over fertilizing can be disastrous, especially with potted plants.

CHAPTER TWENTY
PUTTING ON THE BEAUTY

Forcing bulbs will do much to shorten the seemingly interminable winter season. "Forcing" refers to the practice of planting some bulbs in pots in the fall and bringing them inside for bloom in February and March. Carefully following a few simple steps will ensure success. The mid-winter cheer produced by a pot of yellow and orange daffodils, red and yellow tulips, or hyacinths in their range of startlingly vivid colors from white through pink to blue is impossible to describe. In forcing hyacinths, one should be aware that their fragrance when in bloom is exceedingly strong indoors. For some people it is utterly delightful; for others it may be overpowering.

I begin in late September by filling eight or ten-inch pots with good potting soil, perhaps enriching each with a half cup or so of dehydrated or well-composted livestock manure, bonemeal, and, if I have it available, as much leaf mold. Cover the drainage holes in the pot with shard; drainage must be good. Fill it to within two inches of the top with a good potting mix and plant the bulbs no more than an inch apart, but without touching. Cover them with the potting mix so that tips are barely visible. It is wise to make sure the variety one is using will respond to forcing; some won't. Catalogs as well as the local nurseryman will identify those. One shouldn't be niggardly in the number of bulbs put in a pot—a nice full effect is best.

The bulbs need to grow outdoors in the pots a couple months before the ground freezes for good root development. Water the planted pots well and place them in the ground within a cold frame or protected garden area. Dig a trench deep enough so that the pots can be well covered. Several inches of Canadian peat moss make a good covering, topped with a mulch of leaves. A covering of soil will freeze and make the task of retrieving them difficult. If rodents are a threat, cover the pots with hardware cloth or screening, making sure ample water can get to them. Put stakes or other markers by each pot so they can be located quickly in mid-winter.

The pots can be retrieved at two-week intervals beginning mid-January. I bring ours into our attached garage or some area where the temperature hovers from forty to fifty degrees. The tender white sprouts an inch or so long need to be slowly acclimated to light. As soon as they turn green, place them in the sunlight of a south window or in as well-lighted area as is available. Watered well, they grow rapidly and come into bloom within a month. The cooler they are kept when in bloom, the longer they will last. Any temperature above seventy degrees is disastrous for them, just as is the case in the spring garden.

Being myself of the niggardly sort, I cannot bring myself to throw out the bulbs when the blooms are spent. I remove the blooming stocks and plant the bulbs outside in the spring, hoping they will grow and bloom in a succeeding season. Sometimes they do, sometimes not, but at least I have given them a chance.

Branches of spring blooming shrubs and trees may also be forced into early bloom for the home. Forsythia is one of the easiest. Branches of pussy willow and flowering quince respond readily, and one may also bring in branches of such trees as flowering crab apple and cherries. A danger, of course, in gathering them is that of marring the natural symmetry of the shrub or tree, but with care one can snip branches that perhaps should be pruned anyway. They should be cut (diagonally, just above a bud) to whatever length is appropriate for the vase being used and the bottom ends split once or twice with a sharp knife for perhaps an inch. This allows the branch to readily absorb essential water. Cut them when the temperature is above freezing.

By forcing spring blooming bulbs and shrubs a person brings natural beauty into the home, with all the aesthetic pleasure and deep delight that such beauty yields. One's response to the beauty of a bloom is something more than simply a perception of the senses. G. K. Chesterton wrote: ". . . beauty and terror are very real things and related to a real spiritual world, and to touch them at all, even in doubt or fancy, is to stir the deep things of the soul." (*The Everlasting Man*, 108) To contemplate a beautiful flower is to catch a glimpse, however fleeting, of the world of spirit.

Something mysterious about any beautiful object arouses a desire for more, a yearning for something beyond that can only be glimpsed through it, together with a provoking inability to explain what it is one is seeking. I feel it each time I see a beautiful bloom. The more captivating the beauty, the deeper the mysterious hunger. It is accompanied with a desire to be clean, to be delivered from all that is crude and base, and to be freed from confining inhibitions. C. S. Lewis describes the feeling in a number of places, seeing it as strong evidence that people were created for a higher destiny and a more complete participation in life itself than this world allows. When contemplating the future of the overcoming Christian, he wrote:

> We are to shine as the sun, we are to be given the Morning Star. I think I begin to see what it means. In one way, of course, God has given us the Morning Star already. . . . Ah, but we want so much more—something that books on aesthetics take little notice of. But the poets and the mythologies know all about it. We do not want merely to see beauty, though, God knows, even that is bounty enough. We want something else which can hardly be put into words—to be united with the beauty we see, to pass into it, to receive it into ourselves, to bathe in it, to become part of it. That is why we have peopled air and earth and water with gods and goddesses and nymphs and elves—that, though we cannot, yet these projections can, enjoy in themselves that beauty, grace, and power of which nature is the image. . . . For if we take the imagery of Scripture seriously, if we believe that God will one day give us the Morning Star and cause us to put on the splendour of the sun, than we may surmise that both the ancient myths and the modern poetry, so false as history, may be very near the truth as prophecy. (*The Weight of Glory*, 12, 13)

"Those who are wise shall shine like the brightness of the firmament; and those who turn many to righteousness, like the stars for ever and ever" (Dan 12: 3). To know this truth is greatly to enhance both one's appreciation of the beauties of flowers and one's awe as regards the imagery of Scripture. For instance, the exquisite objects with which the Bible describes the Heavenly City—precious metals and enchantingly glorious stones—are not ends in themselves but expressions of a beauty in which believers, as "living stones" in the temple of redeemed humanity God is building, will participate.

For the writers of Scripture to have used the imagery of flowers and landscapes would have been to imply a fleeting, ephemeral quality, whereas the imagery of gold and precious stones implies immutability and endurance. David describes Zion as "the perfection of beauty" (Psa. 50:2), and Paul speaks of death as our mortality being "swallowed up by life" (2 Cor. 5: 4). We are at a loss to know what it all will mean in actual experience, but we know the promises of Scripture are "great and precious." God would not have given us the hope He has were there any doubt of its fulfillment. "And hope does not disappoint us," Paul assures (Rom. 5:5). To receive rightly the beauty of a bloom is to make a proper start toward a knowledge of the spirit world the soul is indeed bereft without.

CHAPTER TWENTY ONE
THE UNIMAGINABLE ZERO SUMMER

It's the tenth of February, and the sunlight is reflecting off the snow with an almost blinding glitter. It is two and one half times stronger now than in mid-December, the weather forecaster remarks. He is obviously right. As the days grow noticeably longer, impatience for the arrival of spring steadily mounts. Even though spring, when it does finally arrive, may be less gratifying than its promise, it is a glorious season, especially for the gardener.

Meanwhile, wisdom is to enjoy indoor plants. Stately amaryllis blooms are now at their height, huge trumpets in vivid hues of red, orange, apple-blossom pink, and white. Some of the most compelling are red with a large white star in the center. I potted them in mid-November, with the thought of their being in full bloom during the Christmas holidays, but timing the blooms of plants, whether in the summer garden or in the sun room, has never been among my strong points. One of the thirteen I planted, to be sure, was opening on Christmas day; three bloomed during January; seven are now grouped in glorious display; and two late starters have just recently begun to send up their stalks.

I have had several of these huge bulbs for years, summering them in a shady area to the side of the garden, bringing them in for a three-month rest in early fall, then repotting and arousing them to growth. Having been adequately fertilized throughout the summer, they faithfully give a repeat performance. With reasonable care I will have them for several years.

An amaryllis is easily grown. Simple instructions are included with the bulbs one can readily find in garden centers and discount houses in late fall. A few words of caution may be helpful. Buy bulbs that are firm, never soft; avoid ones that give the slightest indication of beginning rot. If the "kit" includes a plastic pot, discard it; instead plant the bulb in a heavy pot, such as a clay one, about the same size as the discarded one, making sure it has excellent drainage. The blooming stalk with its head of four or more huge trumpet blooms will be heavy, and the chances are great that if a person uses the light plastic pot, it will tumble from its shelf and sprawl broken over the rug at the height of its magnificent display.

Leave no more than an inch of space between the sides of the pot and the bulb. Using the growing medium provided, make a bed in the bottom, gently spread the roots out and pack the medium around the bulb, leaving the top third of the bulb exposed. If you are repotting, use pure peat moss, adding a little sand if it is available.

Set the pot in a tray of tepid water (unsoftened), allowing the bulb to absorb what it will for an hour or so. Do not water from the top. Then place it in a reasonably lighted, warm place. It will be very reluctant to grow if the temperature ever falls below 70 degrees. Gentle bottom heat helps awaken sluggish bulbs. Possible rotting at this stage is a danger; don't water again until you see the first signs of growth. Thereafter, bottom water about twice a week, allowing the bulb to absorb what it will in a half hour. Don't allow it to sit in water over an extended period of time.

After it has finished blooming, cut the now unsightly stalk off and continue the watering regime, using a liquid fertilizer. During the summer I immerse the pots in a trench filled with peat moss or leaf mold in an out-of-the-way spot of light shade in the garden, water them during dry periods, and give them liquid fertilizer every two to four weeks.

About the first of September I take them into a dark area of the basement and lay them on their sides for about twelve weeks in order for the old foliage to turn brown and the bulbs to rest. Around Thanksgiving I repot them and begin the regime all over again. I have kept bulbs for years this way, losing only a few.

The huge, vividly tinted amaryllis blooms both give pleasure during the winter and stimulate the desire to make the next season in the garden better than the last one. Hope, expectation, the longing for the advent of something higher and better are very much a part of what it is to be human. Whatever it is beyond this world that the heart's desire fixes upon, the beauty of flowers here and now mysteriously foreshadows it. Together with a brilliantly sun- lit day in mid-winter, they contain the promise of great things to come.

At the beginning of "Little Gidding", T. S. Eliot describes an unusually warm winter day, as "midwinter spring." The bright sunshine glistening on the snow-filled top of the hedgerow stimulates his longing for the summer ahead. It is symbolic of his yearning for the eternal:

This is the spring time
But not in time's covenant. Now the hedgerow
Is blanched for an hour with transitory blossom
Of snow, a bloom more sudden
Than that of summer, neither budding nor fading,
Not in the scheme of generation.
Where is the summer, the unimaginable
Zero summer?
(*Complete Poems and Plays*, 138)

What a moving image: "the unimaginable zero summer"! It captures in a phrase what all the prophets envision as the consummation of redeemed human experience. "For you who fear my name the sun of righteousness shall rise, with healing in its wings. You shall go forth leaping like calves from the stall." (Mal. 4:2) It is the promised coming of new life, more life, for which the heart craves. The Christian life in this world is, as it were, a February day.

WORKS CITED

Bible. *Revised Standard Version*, 1952. *King James Version*, 1611.

Blake, William. *The Complete Poetry and Prose of William Blake*, rev. ed. Edited by David V. Erdman. Berkley and Los Angles: University of California Press. 1982.

Browning, Robert. *Pippa Passes and Shorter Poems*. Edited by Joseph E. Baker. New York: Odyssey, 1947.

_____. *The Ring and the Book*. London: Oxford University Press, 1912.

Bunyan, John. *The Pilgrim's Progress*. 1678. Edited by N. H. Keeble, Oxford: Oxford University Press, 1991.

Chesterton, G. K. *Orthodoxy*, 1908. Wheaton, IL.: Harold Shaw, 1994.

_____. *The Everlasting Man*. San Francisco: Ignatius Press, 1993.

Dante. *The Comedy of Dante Alighieri: Paradise*. Translated by Dorothy Sayers and Barbara Reynolds. Hammondsworth, Middlesex, England: Penguin Books, 1962.

Dickinson, Emily. *The Complete Poems of Emily Dickinson*. Edited by Thomas H. Johnson. Boston: Little, Brown, 1960.

Dostoyevsky, Fyodor. *The Brothers Karamazov*. Translated by Constance Garnett. New York: The Modern Library, 1950.

Eliot, T. S. *The Complete Poems and Plays: 1909 - 1950*. New York: Harcourt, Brace & World, 1971.

Frost, Robert. *Complete Poems, Prose, & Plays*. Edited by Richard Poirier and Mark Richardson. New York: The Library of America. 1995.

Herbert, George. *Selected Poems of George Herbert*. Edited by Gareth Reeves. New York: Barnes & Noble, 1971.

Hill, Caroline Miles, ed. *The World's Great Religious Poetry*. New York: Macmillan, 1943.

Hopkins, Gerard Manley. *The Poems of Gerard Manley Hopkins*. Eds. , W. H. Gardner and N. H. MacKenzie. London: Oxford University Press, 1967.

Law, William. *A Practical Treatise on Christian Perfection*, 1726. Edited by Erwin Paul Rudolph. Carol Stream, IL.: Creation House, 1975.

Lewis, C. S. *The Weight of Glory*. New York: Macmillan, 1949.

MacDonald, George. *The Poetical Works of George MacDonald*. 2 vols. London: Chatto & Windus, 1893.

_____. *A Book of Strife in the form of the Diary of an Old Soul*. London: Dent & Sons, 1913.

_____. *Donal Grant*, 1883. Whitethorn, CA: Johannesen, 1998.

_____. *The Elect Lady*, 1888. Whitethorn, CA.: Johannesen, 2003.

_____. *Paul Faber*, Surgeon, 1879. Whitethorn, CA: Johannesen, 1998.

_____. *Unspoken Sermons*: Third Series, 1889. Whitethorn, CA.: Johannesen, 1999.

_____. *Weighed and Wanting*, 1882. Whitethorn, CA.: Johannesen, 1996

Masefield, John. *Poems*. New York: Macmillan, 1935.

Milton, John. *Complete Poems and Major Prose*. Edited by Merritt Y. Hughes. New York: The Odyssey Press, 1957.

Muir, Edwin. *Collected Poems: 1921 - 1951*. New York: Grove Press, 1957.

Patmore, Coventry. *The Rod, The Root and the Flower*. New York: Books for Libraries Press, 1968.

Robinson, Edwin Arlington. *Collected Poems*. New York: Macmillan, 1937.

Shakespeare, William. *The Yale Shakespeare: The Tragedy of Hamlet Prince of Denmark*. Edited by Tucker Brooke and Jack Randall Crawford. New Haven: Yale University Press, 1947.

Stevens, Wallace. *The Collected Poems of Wallace Stevens*. New York: Vintage, 1982.

Thomas, Dylan. *The Collected Poems of Dylan Thomas: 1934 - 1952*. New York: New Directions, 1957.

WORKS CITED (cont.)

Tolstoi, L. N. *Resurrection*. 1899 - 1900. Trans. Rosemary Edmonds. London: Penguin Books, 1966.

Updike, John. *Collected Poems: 1953 - 1993*. New York: Alfred Knopf, 1995.

Weil, Simone. *Waiting for God*, 1951. Translated by Emma Craufurd. New York: Perennial Classics-HarperCollins, 2001.

Wordsworth, William. *William Wordsworth*. Edited by Stephen Gill. Oxford: Oxford University Press, 1984.

Yeats, William Butler. *The Collected Poems of* W.B. *Yeats*. New York: MacMillan, 1956.

RECOMMENDED SOURCES

B & D Lilies. P. O. Box 2007, 284566 Hwy 101 S., Port Townsend, WA 98368. http://www.bdlilies.com

Bluestone Perennials. 7211 Middle RidgeRd., Madison, Ohio 44057.
http://www.bluestoneperennials.com

Charley's Greenhouse and Garden. 17979 State Route 536, Mount Vernon WA 98273-3269
http://www.charleysgreenhouse.com

J. I. Rodale, et. al. *The Encyclopedia of Organic Gardening*. Emmaus, PA.

Logee's Greenhouses. 141 North Street, Danielson, CT 06239-1939
http://www.logees.com

Mellinger's Inc. 2310 W. South Range Rd., P. O. Box 157, North Lima, OH 44452
http://www.mellingers.com

Park's Seeds. 1 Parkton Ave., Greenwood, SC 29647-0001
http://www.parkseed.com

Pinetree Garden Seeds. Box 300, New Gloucester, ME 04260
http://www.superseeds.com

Stokes Seeds, Inc. Box 548, Buffalo, NY 14240-0548
http://www.stokeseeds.com

Stokes Tropicals. P. O. Box 9868, New Iberia, LA 70562-9866.
http://www.stokestropicals.com

Wayside Gardens. 1 Garden Lane, Hodges, SC 29695-0001.
http://www.waysidegardens.com

www.ingramcontent.com/pod-product-compliance
Lightning Source LLC
Chambersburg PA
CBHW071443160426
43195CB00013B/2013